THE RESOLUTION
FOR MEN

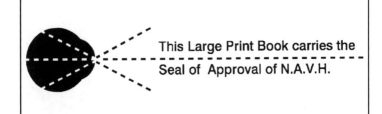

This Large Print Book carries the
Seal of Approval of N.A.V.H.

THE RESOLUTION FOR MEN

STEPHEN & ALEX KENDRICK
with Randy Alcorn
edited by Lawrence Kimbrough

CHRISTIAN LARGE PRINT

A part of Gale, Cengage Learning

Detroit • New York • San Francisco • New Haven, Conn • Waterville, Maine • London

GALE
CENGAGE Learning

LIBRARY OF CONGRESS CATALOGING-IN-PUBLICATION DATA

Kendrick, Stephen, 1973–
    The resolution for men / by Stephen & Alex Kendrick with Randy Alcorn. — Large print ed.
        p. cm. — (Christian Large Print originals)
        Originally published: Nashville : Broadman & Holman, 2011.
        ISBN-13: 978-1-59415-385-3 (softcover)
        ISBN-10: 1-59415-385-X (softcover)
        1. Christian men—Religious life. 2. Large type books. I. Kendrick, Alex, 1970– II. Alcorn, Randy C. III. Title. IV. Series.
    BV4528.2.K46 2011
    248.8'42—dc23   2011029430

Published in 2011 by arrangement with Broadman & Holman Publishers.

Printed in the United States of America
1 2 3 4 5 6 7 15 14 13 12 11

CONTENTS

Weak men will not be able to handle the contents of this book.

The Resolution is not for the faint of heart, and those who commit to it will be more accountable in the future.

You will be challenged to get out of your comfort zone, work through hidden issues from your past, and make strategic sacrifices for the sake of your family and your faith.

But those who step up to the challenge will find that living out the Resolution will radically impact their priorities and assist them in becoming strong men who are found faithful.

It will take courage. But it will be worth it all.

You've been warned.

INTRODUCTION

This book is an unapologetic call for men to live courageously for their faith and their families. It is designed to strategically challenge you to become the man God created you to be.

In the following pages, we will discuss God's uniquely designed journey for a man from birth to death. We will talk about how to let go of the past, become a stronger spiritual leader in your home, win the hearts of your children, and pursue the ironclad character God wants to develop in each of us as men. Finally, we will challenge you to commit to living for God's higher purposes in the form of a *Resolution*.

We want you to experience the rewards that come from fearlessly embracing the responsibilities God has given to all men, regardless of any past mistakes — boldly living the life God intended right now and then leaving a strong legacy for many generations to come.

Too many men sadly waste their lives. They don't really know the God they claim to worship and have not ultimately concluded what they are living for. Halfhearted and indecisive, they spiritually wander through life in a fog of confusion and apathy. They can tell you what they're doing this weekend, but they have no clue about their purpose in life or in eternity. As a result, they go through the motions day after day, wasting most of their time on trivial matters.

At home, men are notorious for being oblivious to the huge leadership vacuum their passivity creates. They don't realize how negatively their wives and children are affected by their lack of spiritual direction and leadership.

But we don't have to keep living this way.

We can be inspired by the fact that great things happen when men wake up and step up. When a man finally understands his role and resolutely surrenders himself to God's plan, his life completely changes. His priorities and vision become clear, and his life takes on a bold new purpose. He learns to say "no" to sinful and secondary things that hold him back, and keep his values and commitments strong no matter the circumstance.

The Old Testament leader Joshua was a man of resolution. He knew who he was and what his responsibilities were. Time and again, his boldness, faith, and courage rallied the fearful, forgetful men of Israel to battle and conquest. Finally, standing before them near the end of his life, delivering a farewell address to his countrymen, his wholehearted resolve and commitment to God as the leader of his family still showed through. He said:

> If it is disagreeable in your sight to serve the LORD, choose for yourselves today whom you will serve: whether the gods which your fathers served which were beyond the River, or the gods of the Amorites in whose land you are living; but as for me and my house, we will serve the LORD. (Joshua 24:15)

He wasn't swayed by what the thousands of men around him decided to do. Whether or not they responded favorably to his challenge did not affect Joshua in the least. Even before they made their decisions, he was already resolute.

"But as for me and my house . . ."

Even if his house was the only one.

Joshua's words rise up from history and echo in our ears today. He asks us, "Where do you stand? Choose today! Stop wallowing and waiting. Stop shifting back and forth, sitting on the fence in your commitments. Make it clear where you stand! What are you waiting for?"

Well, how would you answer that question right now?

What is the status of your resolve compared to Joshua's?

If it falls short, then you have a decision to make. Will you launch out into the deep with God, or will you continue playing games in the shallow end? Are you going to follow the latest popular philosophies and take your chances, or will you wisely start dealing with the real issues of life?

We believe there is a rising movement of men who are disgusted by their own mediocrity and dissatisfied with the weak standards of our dark culture. Men who desire to lock shields with other strong men and step up with courage to stand for Christ and their families like never before. Men who want to make the most of the rest of their days. Men who understand that eternity is too long for them to waste the remainder of their short time here on earth.

Throughout history, men who lived incredible lives and left great legacies did it intentionally. They knew that men do not stumble upon integrity or accidentally find themselves being faithful to God. Passivity merely leads to futility. A man cannot be passive about what Scripture tells him to do for his family and expect to be found faithful to God in the end. He must see with spiritual eyes and realize that future generations are directly impacted by his daily decisions.

God's Word is calling us to "man up!" To be all He's created us to be and do all He's prepared for us to do. We can continue as we are and fail to learn from our mistakes and the mistakes of our ancestors, or we can blaze a new trail of faithfulness for our children and for multiple generations yet to be born. It's time to make some serious decisions.

This is what led us to establish the *Resolution.*

WHAT IS THE *RESOLUTION?*

The *Resolution* is a game changer. It is a bold declaration stating that from this point on, you are choosing to live for what matters most. It's established in your heart and then spoken from your lips, committing yourself to fulfill your God-given responsibilities and live your life with faith and integrity. It expresses who you desire to be as a man and reminds you of your priceless influence on the next generation.

Resolving means deciding — once and for all. The Scriptures describe a resolute man as being *steadfast,* meaning he has chosen to stand up and become fixed on doing what is right. The psalmist describes a blessed man by saying, "His heart is *steadfast,* trusting the LORD" (Psalm 112:7).

A solid, truthful, well-thought-out resolution will redirect the remainder of your days to a finish line marked FAITHFUL so you can run the rest of the race of life with endurance and never turn back.

The *Resolution* statements in this book are based upon the highest priorities for men in God's Word. Each statement describes a commitment you should resolve to live by as the leader of your home. They represent a call to action, and living by them will ultimately help you stand before God one day and hear Him say, "Well done!"

Here is the *Resolution for Men* that we will explain and challenge you to make in the days ahead . . .

THE RESOLUTION

I DO solemnly resolve before God to take full responsibility for myself, my wife, and my children.

I WILL love them, protect them, serve them, and teach them the Word of God as the spiritual leader of my home.

I WILL be faithful to my wife, to love and honor her, and be willing to lay down my life for her as Jesus Christ did for me.

I WILL bless my children and teach them to love God with all of their hearts, all of their minds, and all of their strength.

I WILL train them to honor authority and live responsibly.

I WILL confront evil, pursue justice, and love mercy.

I WILL pray for others and treat them with kindness, respect, and compassion.

I WILL work diligently to provide for the needs of my family.

I WILL forgive those who have
wronged me and reconcile with those
I have wronged.

I WILL learn from my mistakes, repent of
my sins, and walk with integrity as a man
answerable to God.

I WILL seek to honor God, be faithful
to His church, obey His Word,
and do His will.

I WILL courageously work with the
strength God provides to fulfill this
resolution for the rest of my life and
for His glory.

As for me and my house, we will serve
the LORD.

Joshua 24:15

The points in this *Resolution* are key things God has commanded us to do in Scripture, and we should take them very seriously. This is not a list of short-range goals to consider. It's not a decision you make on New Year's Day and lay aside within a few weeks. This is a life resolution that you commit to, and then *keep* recommitting to for the rest of your days.

You may find, as you read through the list, that you agree with every point stated, but you don't think you're ready to commit to them. That's OK. Scripture says it is better not to make commitments than to make them hastily and then not keep them. But these are not new concepts. They come straight from the Scriptures. And because God has already commanded us to keep these standards, He obviously expects us to live by them.

We are just challenging you to do what God is going to hold each of us accountable for doing anyway. So be confident that with His help, you can become true to these commitments. As you rely on Him, He will provide you with the grace and strength to be faithful to each one.

Still, when you read the *Resolution,* you may feel overwhelmed by a sense of inadequacy, as though your past is a heavy millstone weighing around your neck, holding you back. We have all made countless mistakes. We have all stumbled in many ways. But God's mercy is bigger than our past. And the testimonies of others and the Word of God both show us that it is never too late to start doing the right thing. Past failure doesn't have to mean future failure. If you have failed at these things in the past, you can still grow and become a man of God, proving successful in your roles as a husband, father, and grandfather. The greatest encouragement is knowing that God *wants* you to be successful. He is calling and equipping you!

You may have spent years in anger at the mistakes your own father made, mistakes that have brought great pain into your life. If so, now is the time to deal with the past and start focusing on becoming the father you wish you'd had. We challenge you to develop a hatred for mediocrity in your commitments and to spit out any half-hearted efforts as if they were lukewarm water. We are praying for breakthroughs as you read this book, hoping that a fresh surge of spiritual adrenaline will drive you to fully embrace all that God is calling you to be and do.

We recognize that the wording of the

Resolution does not apply to all men who will read this book. We commend those of you who are single, who have come here because you want to better understand and prepare for being a husband and father in the days ahead. You may be married with no children yet, and you want to be better at leading your wife. You may have children but no spouse, and you desire to better understand and succeed in your role as a dad. You may be a grandfather wanting to maximize your influence and redeem this season of your life.

Whether you are married or not, or have children or not, we invite you to take on the challenge. Apply the *Resolution* to your situation, and join us in embracing God's call to become godly men who are stepping up as spiritual leaders in this generation.

Signing this resolution will be easy and take seconds. But fully living it out and being true to its principles will be difficult and take the rest of our lives. We are aware of this. This is why it is good to do this with other men and to maintain accountability. In fact, we've added discussion questions at the end of the book, as well as a memory verse and specific challenge at the end of each chapter, to help you get the most out of this experience.

But be sure of this: whatever way you choose to go about it, every chapter in this book is a strategic investment in you to help you win. We are inviting you to be *courageous* — to learn what it means to become a man of firm resolution. We fully intend to give ourselves to this and are asking God to help us intentionally pursue the kind of lives that are found faithful to Him in the end. And we are asking you to join us on this incredible journey.

As men, we are called to this! We were made for this!

And by God's grace we can do this! It's time to *man up!*

Be alert; stand firm in the faith; act like men; be strong. (1 Corinthians 16:13)

■ ■ ■ ■

PART ONE:
A CALL TO MEN

■ ■ ■ ■

He will restore the hearts of the fathers to their children, and the hearts of the children to their fathers, so that I will not come and smite the land with a curse.

Malachi 4:6

CHAPTER 1
WHY WE NEED
MEN OF RESOLUTION

Awake, sleeper, and arise from the dead,
and Christ will shine on you. Therefore be
careful how you walk, not as unwise men
but as wise, making the most of your
time, because the days are evil.
Ephesians 5:14–16

When Jack woke up to people screaming, he was jolted back into reality, and it took him only a split second to realize this wasn't a dream. His wife, Sarah, had reached over to try steering their minivan back onto the road, but she had overcompensated, swerving past their lane and into oncoming traffic. A guy in a pickup truck laid on his horn and quickly maneuvered off the road, barely missing them.

"Watch out!" Jack yelled as he once again grabbed the wheel. But Sarah's hands still gripped it tightly as she swung their vehicle back across the lane to the right, again overcorrecting and veering them off the road on the other side. The rapid thumping of the road deflectors under the tires was soon replaced by the sound of guardrails scraping down the side of their van. Jack flinched as a road sign quickly took out the right, sideview mirror. All three of their children in the back seat began crying hysterically as the car sped toward a sharp turn in the road, where a single railing was the only thing keeping them from plummeting over a dirt embankment.

"Let go, Sarah! I got it!"

Everything went into slow motion. Jack, in shock, turned to his wife, who was pale white with a look of intense fear in her eyes, hands fused to the wheel as she and her husband both fought — almost against each other — to control the car's path. His eyes darted up to the rearview mirror to see the panic-stricken faces of the children he loved more than any others in the world. Reality began settling into Jack's mind: he had fallen asleep at the wheel. He knew that he was the reason why his whole family was about to die. But he also knew that the cause of their current crisis was the key to their potential rescue.

Himself.

With a knee-jerk reaction, Jack hit the

brakes, sending the car sliding on the pavement, throwing everyone's body forward, locking their seatbelts around them like a vise. Burning out the tires, he screeched to a halt within inches of the guardrail overlooking the long drop-off. As everyone rocked backward and into their seats, Jack stared over the hood in shock at the catastrophe his entire family had been mere seconds from experiencing.

His wife and kids were speechless. Jack sat silently, repressing an emotional rush of guilt mixed with relief. Sarah unlocked her seatbelt, wrapped her arms around him, and buried her head into his chest, sobbing in relief. His children also continued to cry as Jack whispered, "I'm so sorry; I'm so sorry" — over and over again.

Fear. Gratitude. Trauma. Prayer. Sarah cycled through every emotional response in her system. She was still a mess, very slowly starting to pull herself back together. Then finally, with her heart rhythm beginning to lessen, color returning to her cheeks, she looked up at Jack through tear-filled eyes and whispered words he would never forget: "Please don't ever do that again."

This vivid story illustrates where countless men are today. Disengaged and drifting. They have been given the position of leadership over their families and have been placed in the driver's seat. But over time, they have been lulled into a dream by their own passivity and the allures of a dark, seductive culture.

In this dream world, men often feel permission to be irresponsible, immature, and carelessly negligent in their roles as husbands and fathers. In the meantime, they have placed their families in moral and spiritual danger, threatening their marriages, their children, and their faith. They don't realize that they can't have it both ways.

As a result, the mothers of their children become the ones who (by default and necessity) are carrying the weight of the family on their shoulders in order to survive. These women are stressed out and longing for the man in their lives to wake up, rescue them, and grab the wheel again.

That's why before it's too late, we are sounding the call and asking men if they are awake at the wheel. Or more importantly, to see if they even realize they are in the driver's seat at all.

God's Word commands husbands and fathers to lovingly lead their homes. As men, we are to walk in honor and integrity and fully embrace our responsibilities as shepherds over our families. We are called to model a loving, Christlike example for our wives and children.

Therefore — because this is God's calling — it's no mystery that a godless culture would mock and constantly undermine fatherhood, attacking and inverting what God designs and values. Men are being told they don't have the permission or responsibility to lead. But the culture is not your authority. *God is.*

You need to be willing to ask yourself some revealing questions:

- Is your wife weary, worn out, and always feeling like she is carrying too much on her shoulders?
- Does your marriage lack clear direction, romance, and true intimacy?
- Are your children, whether young or grown, emotionally distant from you and spiritually apathetic toward God?
- Is your own faith and spiritual condition weak or mediocre at best?

If your wife has been calling all the shots in the family and has her hands on the wheel, then very likely it's because you have not. Regardless of what she does, God has intentionally placed *you* in the driver's seat and wants *you* to lead. You need her deeply; but leading is your God-ordained responsibility, not hers.

You may not like this. You may feel totally inadequate in your leadership of your home. You may not see any way to reestablish relationships that have slipped into brokenness and distrust. Like countless men, you may have huge regrets and valid obstacles that seem to keep you from being the man you want to be inside.

Be encouraged! We want to give you some very real hope and direction toward future success in your journey. No man and no family is a lost cause when God gets involved. And since you are also the one in the driver's seat, you can become the one He uses to steer your family back onto the path that will lead them to a place of safety, strength, and health.

All of us should be willing to go to the next level. When you get right down to it, the success or failure of fatherhood is the key issue of our generation. *Leadership determines direction.*

And deep down inside, we all know it.

And we all really want things to improve.

THE POWER OF A FATHER

If you want to get to the core of who people really are, get them to start talking about their dad. Let them tell you what he said to them. How he treated them. Things he modeled for them. It will be very telling as to *why* they are *who* they are. And if they're being transparent, they will often be fighting back tears, either because they loved and admired their father so much or because he deeply wounded them in one or more ways.

Regardless of age, everyone wants a good answer to the question, "What does my dad really think about me?" Our hearts intrinsically long for his approval. And when we don't get it, we tend to spend the rest of our lives working tirelessly to win the approval of others in an attempt to fill the intense void he has left. At the same time, when a man becomes bitter with his father, he can spend his whole life trying to prove his dad wrong. He'll say, "I never want to be like my dad." Either way, his dad becomes the focus of so much emotional energy in his life.

But a lot of fathers don't realize their vital role, and their kids are destined to suffer for it. If you boil down many of the issues associated with today's detached, passive, or absentee dads, you discover this: *fathers have lost their sense of purpose.*

Dads used to be very intentional about *fathering* their children. They knew how pivotal their influence was. But because so many fathers today don't know who they are or what they are doing, they end up doing very little. And because they are not training their sons how to be responsible men, the culture is stepping in and subtly emasculating them.

This current generation of young men doesn't know what it means to be a man. Or to be a mature, responsible leader. Or to be a strong and engaged father one day. Society is guiding boys to remain boys as long as possible — extending childhood into their thirties — while forcing girls to become women long before they are ready.

Instead of growing up, getting married, and courageously raising up the next generation, millions of young men are staying single, remaining emotionally and directionally dependent on their mothers while becoming addicted to entertainment, pornography, and video games. They want the privileges and rewards of manhood but only the responsibilities and moral requirements of boys. So when they become fathers themselves, they don't know what to do, and they feel extremely ill-equipped.

Young women, likewise, are entering life without a deep sense of value and worth. Rather than displaying feminine charm, modesty, and grace, many have become nearly (if not equally) as rude and unrestrained as the stereotypical guy. They are told to act like and outdo men as much as possible. Flirty, immodest, and aggressive, they stay on a constant search for acceptance and attention — things they haven't been freely given by the one man in their life whose love and approval they really want. And so millions of teenage girls auction away their priceless virginity every year for a pizza, a movie, and some on-the-spot flattery. Each of them hopes that being held for a few minutes by a porn-addicted teenage boy with raging hormones will somehow fill the dark canyon of love that her disengaged father has left aching inside her heart. And it never does.

The consistently missing piece of the puzzle? *Fathers.*

THE MISSING PIECE

When a father disconnects, leaves, or dies too soon, so does a part of his child's heart. At the point a child gets detached from his or her father, it creates a massive vacuum of unmet needs in all the key areas for which the father is responsible.

More and more kids are going to bed at night without their father in their home. The physical absence of fathers is now considered the most significant family and social problem facing America.[1]

The research is staggering. Prisoners, drug users, dropouts, runaways, and rapists all share something in common. The overwhelming majority of them come from homes without a father. Fatherless homes produce more than half of all youth suicides, as well as the majority of kids with behavior disorders. Kids are twenty times more likely to end up in prison if their dad is not involved in their lives.[2]

Fatherlessness also affects kids' physical health. Those living without their dads have a much higher rate of asthma, headaches, anxiety, depression, and behavior problems. They are significantly more likely to use drugs and become suicidal.[3]

It makes sense, then, why the Scripture says God has a special place in His heart for two specific groups of people: *fatherless children* and *widows*. In James 1:27, the Bible describes "pure and undefiled religion" in terms of visiting and showing compassion to these individuals in their "distress." What do fatherless children and widows have in common? The most important man in the leadership role of their lives is gone.

Even the dads who have every intention of doing a better job in this role are finding a world of things working against them, luring them away from their leadership mission. There are multiple factors undermining fatherhood. Here are some of the most influential.

Divorce. Marriage is the glue that keeps dads connected to their children. Illegitimate births and divorce are the two greatest factors that steal kids away from their fathers. Couples in previous generations were more likely to stay together for the sake of the kids. But this generation has been increasingly convinced that kids are better off if their unhappy parents get a divorce. The stats reveal that this is not true. The absolute best thing for kids is to see their parents humble themselves, repent of their selfishness, forgive one another, and recommit to their marriage. The convenience of no-fault divorce has come at an extremely high price. And millions of innocent kids are forced to pay that price every year.

Work. Before the industrial revolution, fathers primarily worked at home with their children often working alongside *them,* giving dads natural opportunities for sharing their faith and their values with the next generation. But in the 1800s, factory work took men away from home, leaving kids alone with mom and diminishing the influence of fathers. When dad finally did get home, he was too tired to engage, and his family got the leftovers of his attention and energy. Today, the problem continues. If a man doesn't set boundaries and learn to say "no," his work priorities will constantly pull him away from his wife and children whose hearts are reaching for him.

Entertainment. Men today spend more time watching TV or surfing the Internet than in meaningful conversation with their children. If his children are with dad while he's being entertained, then the television becomes their influence instead. And it is a lousy father.

Anti-fatherhood bias in media. When America was guided more by a Judeo-Christian ethic, fathers in television shows and movies were usually depicted as honorable and heroic. In the 1950s and '60s, programs like *Father Knows Best, The Andy Griffith Show, My Three Sons,* and *Leave It to Beaver* showed strong, intelligent, responsible fathers. In contrast, dads on TV today are incompetent and constantly outwitted by their wives and disrespectful kids. Their perversion and passivity subtly redefine what's normal for fathers and can creep into the expectations we have of ourselves.

The church. It hurts to include this item, but too often pastors have gone silent when it comes to teaching men what God's Word says about their roles and responsibilities. At the same time, many church programs separate families to the point that kids never see their fathers leading, reading their Bibles, worshipping, or praying because they're not with them when they do.

These aren't the only threats. From the feminist movement's constant attack on male leadership, to abortion laws that legally identify mothers as solely responsible for the life of their children, to welfare laws that pay moms to keep dad out of the house, men are up against a society that wants to take them down.

Which shouldn't surprise us.

The Devil will never stop attacking what God prioritizes. And just like on a battle-field, the enemy always tries to take out the leader. If you want to keep a team out of the Super Bowl, put their quarterback out of commission. How do you win at chess? By putting the king in checkmate. An all-out assault has been declared against you as a husband and father. And that's why now more than ever, we need men of resolution who understand their purpose.

THE PRICELESS PURPOSE OF FATHERHOOD

God created fatherhood with an eternal purpose: to reveal and represent Himself. He did not simply realize that earthly fathers were like Him and then decide to call Himself our Father. On the contrary, He eternally existed as God the Father in heaven and intentionally created the role of fatherhood on earth to reveal who He is and to show us the nature of His relationship with His Son.

All fatherhood comes from Him (Ephesians 3:14–15). Every human father is called to be a daily, physical representation of God to his children, to introduce Him to the next generation. When a child looks at his earthly father, he should be able to see these qualities of God:

- a loving Provider
- a strong Protector
- a truthful Leader
- a respectable Authority
- an intimate Friend

This affects how a child thinks. "If my earthly father loves and cares for me, then my heavenly Father loves and cares for me. If my father means what he says, then *God* means what He says. If my father would die for me, *God* would die for me." On the other hand, if a child's earthly father is harsh or distant, what will the child think when someone says, "God is your Father"?

Naturally, all of us earthly fathers are unavoidably flawed. We are a long way from being like God. And yet it is part of children's human nature to judge what they *cannot* see in God in light of what they *can* see in us.

Right now, this generation doesn't know what true fatherhood looks like. They rarely see it modeled in the media or at home. And sadly, the result is another generation deeply struggling to understand what God is really like.

The word *father* means "founder, source, chief, or leader." The father of a nation, an invention, a company, or a movement is the one who helped bring it into existence. As our heavenly Father, God is the source from which all other things come into being. In Scripture, God as Father is the first Person of the Trinity. Any time you hear the God-head described, it is always God the Father first, then the Son, then the Holy Spirit. Jesus the Son willingly follows the leadership of the Father. And if you study the life of Christ, you discover that He always speaks the words, performs the works, and carries out the will of His heavenly Father. As God's Son, Jesus came to reveal the Father to us. The Bible says that Jesus is the "fullness" of the Godhead "in bodily form" (Colossians 2:9). So if you want to know what God is like, then just look at Jesus. He represents His Father perfectly.

How well are *you* representing your heavenly Father? To *your* son? To *your* daughter? That is your priceless purpose.

Both the Scriptures and statistics clearly communicate that there is no more influential person in the life of a child than his or her father. Whereas moms are priceless, irreplaceable, and needed beyond measure, they were never designed to be men or to fill the role of a dad. When the Bible states that "the glory of children is their father" (Proverbs 17:6 NKJV), it is revealing an important dynamic of how God has wired the hearts and minds of children.

They learn their identity from you. When your kids are young, they don't know who they are, what is right or wrong, or who God is. They don't know how to live life. But kids naturally go to their dads for answers to their biggest questions: *Who is God? Who am I? Am I loved? Am I a success? Do I have what it takes? What is my purpose in life?* And if dads don't teach their kids the truth about these things, then the world will teach them lies.

They learn their values from you. Kids watch their dads to find what's important. It's a dad's job to keep his children from having to learn the lessons of life the hard way. A father's wise words and actions constantly reinforce the higher priorities and deeper truths of life. So if he is not there — or if he's there but not intentional in his training and leadership — his kids will be walking through their most important decisions without the one person who should be loving and leading them the most.

They learn their worth from you. When a child has a dad who says, "I love you, I'm proud of you, and I'm going to stand with you and always be there for you," it changes the life of that child forever. Sons who have their dads in their lives do significantly better in school, have better social skills and self-esteem, and are more likely to say no to criminal behavior.[4] Similarly, when a daughter looks into the mirror, she needs to hear her father's voice in her heart reminding her that she is beautiful and loved. As a result, girls with strong dads are much more likely to feel secure — and are much *less* likely to have eating disorders and identity issues or to become sexually active in their teen years.[5] But in too many families, this is not what's happening.

We need to rediscover God's original intention of what our homes are supposed to be like. Families should be havens of love and enjoyment. Homes should be places of peace and purpose. But great homes don't just happen. They are gardens that need to be intentionally cultivated and guarded. A man must let truth, love, and wise discipline become constant ingredients to his fathering. He should carefully nurture his wife, his children, and his own attitude so that his home is a place where his marriage and the next generation can grow and thrive.

That's why we need a game-changing *Resolution*.

And that's what our times are calling for.

IT'S TIME FOR MEN TO BE COURAGEOUS

Our generation desperately needs courageous men to step up. We need men who will not be swayed by the culture or afraid of criticism. We need men who are resolved to lead their families no matter what. We need men to teach sexual purity to their sons and daughters so that more children won't enter the world without married parents. We need men who stick to their marriage vows and cry out for God's help to love their wives rather than giving up during difficult times.

We need men who refuse to sacrifice their families for the sake of a promotion at work. Men who refuse to let entertainment eat up all their time and deaden their consciences. Men who will speak out against laws and philosophies that are destroying families. Men who will forgive their dads, break the chains of the past, and set new standards. Men who will pray for their pastors and for revival in their churches and make decisions that will strengthen the next generation. We need to be these men. And we need one another!

When strong men work together, they can accomplish amazing things.

A story from 2 Samuel 10 provides a powerful picture of how we men can effectively support one another in our generation. The armies of David had come together to face their enemies amid seemingly impossible odds. Joab, David's commanding general, recognized that the battle was against him both in front and in the rear. But he and his brother, Abishai, decided to work together, support one another, and then trust God's power, knowing the results were in His hands.

Joab challenged his brother with these bold words:

If the Arameans are too strong for me, then you shall help me, but if the sons of Ammon are too strong for you, then I will come to help you. Be strong, and let us show ourselves courageous for the sake of our people and for the cities of our God; and may the LORD do what is good in His sight. (2 Samuel 10:11–12)

Their gutsy strategy worked! God blessed their courage and teamwork and brought a powerful victory in the midst of what seemed to be an impossible situation.

Men today are feeling intense pressure all around them. The dark depravity of our culture and the desperate needs of the next generation stand in front of us. The mistakes of our fathers and the sins of our own past stand against us from behind. Each of these can feel like an ominous cloud, challenging us to give up and surrender ourselves and our families in defeat.

But we need to remember one immovable, unconditional truth: we have a Father in heaven who is for us — our loving Provider, our strong Protector, our truthful Leader, our respectable Authority, and our intimate Friend. He loves us unconditionally. He alone is a majority, and the battle always belongs to Him!

If He is for us, it doesn't matter who or what is against us.

We are here on this earth at this moment to be like His Son, Jesus Christ. We are here to boldly speak the words, do the work, and carry out the will of our Father. Regardless of what our culture says, regardless of what other men do, we must be courageous to lead our marriages and our families for the sake of the One we represent and for the sake of the generations that will come after us.

We must stop complaining about where our culture is going and resolve instead to do something about it. We must lock shields with other men around us and refuse to allow one another to fail any longer in the battles for our marriages and families. We must give our sons and grandsons a new picture of leadership and a new example worth following. We must help our generation of men to step up to embrace their responsibilities before God and to love and lead their families. If we will take courage and lead the way, we can change the world and leave a strong legacy for our children's children.

That is the purpose of this book. That is our mission!

We must learn to stand up together, become men of resolution, and boldly say, "If my battle gets too strong for me, then you shall help me, but if your battle is too strong for you, then I will come to help you! Be strong, and let us show ourselves courageous for the sake of our people and for the cities of our God; and may the Lord do what is good in His sight!"

COURAGEOUS CHALLENGE

Watch or read out loud the closing speech from the movie *Courageous* (found in the appendix, page 421).

MEMORY VERSE

Be strong, and let us show ourselves courageous for the sake of our people and for the cities of our God; and may the LORD do what is good in His sight.
(2 Samuel 10:12)

I will open my mouth in a parable; I will utter dark sayings of old, which we have heard and known, and our fathers have told us. We will not hide them from their children, telling to the generations to come the praises of the LORD.

Psalm 78:2–4 (NKJV)

CHAPTER 2
A LIFELONG VISION
OF FATHERHOOD

The eyes of the LORD are everywhere,
keeping watch on the wicked
and the good.
Proverbs 15:3 NIV

Imagine that you are sleeping one night, and God visits you in a dream. He says, "Come with Me. I want to show you something." In an instant you find yourself in a dark and dirty room you've never seen before. Glancing around, you see piles of soiled clothes and garbage everywhere. The stench is almost unbearable. Suddenly you see movement in the shadows — a feeble, old man, crouched in a corner alone, gasping for air, and then vomiting on the floor. Disgusted, you turn to the Lord and ask, "Who is that?"

He says, "I want you to consider this man — Timothy — for there are many like him on the earth. He is a wicked and foolish man like his father was, hating Me and always turning toward evil."

God then begins showing you vivid moments throughout the time line of Timothy's life, from beginning to end. You become aware of his illegitimate conception, his unwanted birth, and the poverty and pain resulting from his father's negligence, rejection, and abuse. You see the hurt in Timothy's eyes as a child. His heart gradually fills with anger, then hardens with bitter hatred, then rages with wholehearted rebellion. You shake your head as you watch him grow up to reject all manner of wisdom and warning that God mercifully sends into his life to rescue him, rebelling against every authority, scorning every loving rebuke, resisting repeated invitations to turn his life around.

You can't help but look away as he violates the purity of several young girls during his youth. Daring to turn back, you see the expected results as he fathers, abuses, and then abandons his own children throughout the years.

You witness Timothy repeatedly stealing, squandering, leading others astray, rejecting all forms of responsibility, and taking greedy advantage of others. Always running from the truth, his is a life of violence, perversion, addictions, and drunkenness. And though tormented cruelly by his demons, he responds by raising his fist against God, cursing His name, and recklessly living out his days destroying his own life as well as those around him.

Each decade unfolds before you like one nightmare after another, each with increasingly greater consequences — a rising wake of destruction that ripples out over time, bringing nothing but pain and suffering to the people in his path. He squanders every day of his existence like diamonds slipping through his fingers until his biography finally runs out and catches up to his present heartbeat — the way you first saw him — old, dirty, and degraded beyond recognition.

As you watch him now wallowing on the floor, you see the emptiness and evil in his eyes and become fully aware that the "wages" of Timothy's sin is "death" in every area of his life. Here in his final chapter, you share in God's righteous anger while mourning the loss of what could have been.

Then the Lord speaks again.

"Tomorrow, on his sixty-sixth birthday, the days of my mercy for Timothy will end, and I will require of him his sinful and unrepentant life. He will die here alone, and no one will mourn his passing."

"What then?" you ask.

"He has rejected Me and the offering of My Son, and he will be judged according to the standards of My holy Word. He will be cast into outer darkness to join his fathers in torment." You tremble as you hear these words, but feel a heightened awareness of God's perfect justice knowing it is righteously executed.

You ask, "What good could come from my seeing this man's life, Lord?"

The grief on God's countenance begins to change into hope. He looks into your eyes, and a warm smile awakens on His face. "I want to show you what My grace can do."

"What do you mean?"

"You have seen where Timothy is. Now I want you to experience his life as he *should* have lived it, as if he and his father had both obeyed me completely. You understand that the wages of sin leads to death. But I want you to know the results of righteousness as well."

Instantly you travel with the Lord many decades back in time and find yourself standing in the back of an old country church as the service is concluding. As you gaze around the one-room building, the clothes of those in the congregation remind you of those your great-grandparents wore in photos you had seen as a child. Your attention is drawn to a young man with a crew cut in a military uniform sitting on the back row. He is whispering into the ear of a somewhat scantily dressed young woman seated next to him.

"Who is that, Lord?" you ask.

"That is Timothy's father, James, when he was a young man. Today was the day he hardened his heart and walked away from Me. But you will see him respond differently to My grace in this vision."

Suddenly the rising voice of the guest preacher echoes from behind the pulpit: "Repent, and believe on the Lord Jesus Christ and be saved!" As he passionately calls on everyone "with ears to hear" to turn from their sin, the congregation stands, and the small choir begins to sing the first stanza of "Amazing Grace." Your eyes fix on James as he crosses his arms and clenches his jaw, stone-faced. But then something happens. His countenance changes. He lowers his eyes, thinking soberly. He looks up again, watching people slip one-by-one from their seats and approach the front of the church, kneeling to pray, hungry to get right with God.

"Now is the day of salvation," the preacher

pleadingly declares. "Jesus said, 'Come to Me, all who are weary and heavy-laden, and I will give you rest. Take My yoke upon you and learn from Me, for I am gentle and humble in heart, and you will find rest for your souls.' Repent therefore and be converted, that your sins may be blotted out, so that times of refreshing may come from the presence of the Lord. Come to Christ while you still have the chance! It is time for you to choose."

James begins to tremble and wipe tears from his eyes. Then contrary to anything he had done in the past, he too steps out, slowly walks to the prayer altar near the front of the church, and kneels down. All other sounds in the room fade in the distance, and you can hear every word of his humble prayer. There is so much sincerity in his voice as he cries out to God for help. For forgiveness. He prays to be saved and expresses his faith in the death of God's Son. Then after a brief moment of silence, James stands up and sighs deeply. As he turns and walks back to his seat, you see a difference in his countenance. Something that wasn't there before. Peace and hope.

And you become consciously aware that everything once established about this young man's future is about to unfold in a very different way.

Time races. Your mind begins to flood with images of James's life as his story is rewritten before your eyes. Rather than violating Lilly, the young girl seated next to him on the back row of the church, then abandoning her with Timothy in her womb, you see James share his newfound faith with her instead. She soon embraces his faith as her own, and they talk with the pastor and are both baptized. With childlike belief they begin rebuilding their relationship with a renewed commitment to purity, honor, and sincere love. You watch James talk with Lilly's father, and then marry her with the complete support of their parents and their new church home.

You see them launch into married life with God's blessing and a strong foundation of faith. Every week, James and Lilly grow spiritually as they worship God, listen to the teaching of His Word, fellowship with other believers, and spend time alone in prayer. While reading the Bible one morning, James learns that he is to love his wife like Jesus loves the church. He realizes that God has called him to be the spiritual leader of his home and prays for God to show him what that means. And the more he obeys the Scriptures, the more James matures spiritually and his mind is renewed.

He begins to discern what is right and wrong in his life and also in the example his own parents left him while he was growing up. Having been wounded deeply by his father, you see James battle with his resentment and then completely forgive his dad from his heart. This brings an incredible new freedom from bitterness that had haunted him since his youth. He then asks God to break any destructive chains remaining in his life that had been passed down from his family's history. You feel his joy and liberation as God begins giving him personal breakthroughs on a consistent basis.

James and Lilly establish better habits and begin new family traditions in their home. Sundays become days of rest and worship. They begin making all of their major decisions together in prayer. When disagreements and hurts arise, they quickly work through them and forgive each other. James listens more lovingly to Lilly's ideas and requests, and she increasingly respects and trusts his leadership decisions.

Then it happens. After months of asking God to bless them with children, you hear Lilly announce to James that she is pregnant. Thrilled beyond measure, James thanks God for this priceless gift. He and Lilly begin to pray daily for the Lord to bless, protect, and use this child for His honor. You watch with intrigue as you see the significant difference in Timothy's beginnings from what you had seen in the earlier vision from his life. He is now being born into a strong, God-honoring family where his mother and father deeply love him and one another.

Your mind jumps ahead to see James and Lilly bringing Timothy before their church family and dedicating him to God. You feel their shared sense of inadequacy as they pray with their pastor for the daily wisdom and guidance to raise Timothy well and to train him in the way he should go. You smile as James looks in wonder at his son's tiny face and holds him proudly in his arms.

As you see Timothy grow, you can tell he feels emotionally secure and knows he is loved. You see the amazing balance of a child's mom and dad teaming up together each day to give their son the kind of solid upbringing he needs. His mother's comfort and warnings, matched with his father's encouragement and discipline, develop a loyal and loving respect in his heart for them. He hears his father reading the Scriptures aloud at home and discovers at an early age that God created him in His image and wants to have a relationship with him.

You enjoy watching James wrestle with his son on the floor, teach him how to tie his shoe, and ride a bicycle. You see him carry Timothy on his shoulders around town. "This is my son! He's a great little champ, isn't he?" Many of the things James says or does for Timothy are now inspired by what he wished he had experienced from his own dad while growing up.

As Timothy grows, you observe James using the Ten Commandments to show him right from wrong and how to treat others. Later, you see Timothy later convicted of his selfishness and disobedience as his father explains to him that the "wages of sin is death, but the gift of God is eternal life through Jesus Christ our Lord." Timothy sits wide-eyed in wonder when he hears his dad describe the amazing sacrifice Jesus made willingly on a cross in order to pay for our sins.

Then you later see Timothy — with child-like faith — give his heart and submit his life to Jesus Christ in prayer. You share in the joy of watching him being baptized in their church.

His parents see a clear change in him over

the next few months. His conscience becomes tender. His willingness to obey grows. His longing to love God and others increases.

James is always there to keep Timothy growing in a godly direction, using the events of every day to teach his son character and the lessons of a responsible life. While driving past a homeless man sleeping on the street, he challenges him with the importance of working hard while also showing compassion for the poor. Both at home and at church, he shows him how to open the door for a lady and to stand in the presence of the elderly. After a thief breaks into their house while they are away, he shares with Timothy lessons about forgiveness, honesty, and why we lay up our treasures in heaven.

One day, Timothy walks in the kitchen to see his father holding and kissing his mother. You smile as you watch James turn and wink at Timothy. "Son, when you get married, don't forget to kiss your wife and tell her you love her every day. It will help her stay beautiful like Mommy!" Timothy decides, even as an eight-year-old, that he wants to grow up and get married to someone with a radiant countenance like his mother. Though he realizes more and more that his parents are imperfect and often fail one another, he sees them quickly work through their differences together, forgive, and learn from each mistake.

Several years later, James takes his son along on a business trip. And during their long drive, he explains to him the facts of life. You hear James emphasize with wisdom and care the importance of living with sexual purity. He explains how to treat a young lady as someone's future wife rather than the object of lust for him to undress with his eyes.

"Did you and Mom sin in that way before you got married?" Timothy asks.

You can see the grief on James's face. "Yes, son, I'm sad to say we did. You can't imagine, though, how badly we wish we hadn't. But after we became Christians, we stopped doing that and made our sexual relationship something beautiful again by saving it until our marriage, like God's Word commands."

James pauses to let this sink in, then adds a personal charge forged from his own experience: "You have to keep special things special, son. Don't treat the holy and priceless things of life like they're common and cheap. I want you to learn from our mistakes so you can avoid them. I want you to be able to tell your children that you kept yourself pure until your wedding day out of your obedience to God and your love for your wife."

"Yes sir, I will," Timothy replies. And you know he means it.

This heart-to-heart, man-to-young-man moment begins to define how they interact with each other as Timothy grows, making him desire to live up to his dad's example and expectations. You see Scriptures being read with James's eyes and then quickly spoken into the ears of his son. When Timothy is alone, you hear the words of his father echo in his memory and counsel him during his decisions.

"Keep your promises no matter how hard, son. And be faithful with the little things, especially when no one is watching."

"Treat everyone you meet with kindness, respect, and compassion."

"Know what you believe, why you believe it, and be ready to defend it."

"Do your work with all your heart and with excellence as unto the Lord, not men."

"Be willing to stand alone for what's right regardless of what your friends do or say."

Timothy continues to see in James the kind

of man who's "the real deal," people say, a guy who will "give you the shirt off his back." Timothy even picks up his father's love for reading and begins to learn about heroic, honorable men from Scripture and later history. He feels challenged by their stories, not wanting to be as vain, wasteful, and irresponsible as so many of his peers. When he talks with his dad about this, James puts his arm around him and tells him how proud he is of Timothy's maturity and character. This moment prompts the idea: how about if the two of them start memorizing Scripture each week as a way to help them stay challenged and grow stronger together? Timothy loves the idea. It reminds him how much his dad loves him.

It makes him feel like a man.

Then, when Timothy turns fifteen, James takes him through a rite of passage to call him into manhood. James drives Timothy to a campsite where he's asked several other men to come spend a day with them, speaking into Timothy's life about what it means to be a godly man of integrity. Timothy listens, absorbing and cherishing every word.

At the end of the day, after a special outdoor dinner, James stands up in front of their family and friends, turns to his son, and says, "Timothy, you are my beloved son in whom I am well pleased. Today, I acknowledge you as a man. You are fully accountable now to read, obey, and honor God and His Word from this day forward. God has created you for a special purpose and has great things in store for you in the days ahead."

His voice begins to tremble with pride as he finishes.

"And I want everyone to know that I love you, and I am very proud to be your father."

A tear even wells up in your own eye as you hear the passion of a father's heart, freely pouring out unconditional love to his son. James then presents Timothy with a new Bible, as well as a surprise gift — a heavy, gleaming, steel sword — signifying his call to fight the good fight and to stand strong in his faith.

James embraces his son as everyone cheers. You watch the other men gather around Timothy. They join his father in praying over him, boldly asking God to make him a strong, courageous, and successful man throughout his life.

The man God made new at a little country church now has a new, young man of his own.

You feel honored to be here to see it.

After this day, you can tell that Timothy's mind-set changes. He stands taller and walks straighter. He begins to live fueled by his father's blessing, and he quits worrying so much about what others think of him. He starts to study and meditate on the Scriptures more deeply as he follows the example of Christ. He learns that God has not given him a spirit of fear but of power, love, and a sound mind. He resolves to diligently seek out and do the will of God for His life.

Time flashes by as you see Timothy step up into manhood, do well in his education, surround himself with wise friends, and excel in employment. Wherever he works, his supervisors tend to favor him, amazed at how respectful, humble, and dependable he is.

New seasons of his life pass by, highlighted by his marriage to a virtuous young woman. You watch James place his hands on their shoulders and proudly bless their marriage during the rehearsal dinner. You then see Timothy kissing his bride at the marriage altar to the cheers of their families and friends.

Timothy embraces his responsibilities as a Christian husband, becoming a model of what it means to provide, protect, and lead a man's family. He starts his own small company, making a name for himself not only as a smart businessman but as a respected boss who cares about his employees' lives as much as their work, and who treats his clients with fairness and integrity.

You then share his joy as he and his wife begin having children. As a father, Timothy builds upon the legacy his father had instilled in him, shepherding the hearts of his sons and daughters the way James had modeled. You watch how Timothy and his wife carefully work together to pass on a stronger legacy than even he had been given. He realizes that the values he imparts in his children will eventually impact his great-great-grandchildren one day.

Timothy becomes a leader in his church and community. His pastor entrusts responsibilities to him as a solid teacher and spiritual mentor to other families in their fellowship. His children see his commitment to sharing the joys and sorrows of life with other believers in their church. And as his children come to Christ one by one, they develop a deep, personal love for God and are influenced by both their parents and their grandparents.

As Timothy mentors each of his children,

he calls them into adulthood and blesses them with his love, counsel, and support. Family crises are approached with faith instead of fear. Those who misunderstand or mock his family values are prayed for instead of hated. Timothy and his wife lovingly care for and honor his father, James, and his mother, Lilly, as they live out their final years and pass away.

Timothy's sons grow up to become heroic young men of honor. His daughters become wise and virtuous. They each radiate with kindness and are known for their strong faith, inner beauty, and noble character.

Then the seasons change, children get married, and grandchildren arrive. As time passes before your eyes, you see a family reunion filled with joy as a wise, eighty-year-old Timothy commands attention with his touching stories of faith and life's adventures. He is now able to hold and bless his great-grandchildren. All of them know they are loved, enjoying the rewards and security anchored in such a strong heritage of faith.

As the sun sets on Timothy's life, his appointed day arrives, and you see him lying peacefully, dying in his bed. Still loved and loving. Still spiritually strong in the midst of physical weakness. Still blessing others with the counsel of his whispery voice and the light in his eyes. Still faithful to his marriage vows after all these years. Surrounding him now are his loving wife, children, and grandchildren, each supporting him with their presence, encouragement, and prayers. Staring at his warm, weathered face, you can't help but respect this man who is so fulfilled with His life. So grateful for God's blessings on his family. So rich in all the things that matter.

As you consider the full epic of his story, you become fully aware that the "wages" of Timothy's life have brought immeasurable blessing and joy to his family, church, and community. Countless people have been helped by his example, teaching, and counsel. Business and ministry leaders thrive as a result of his strong leadership. Many individuals have come to faith in God because of his testimony and witness. You begin to hear the cheers of heaven celebrate as he takes his last breath in peace and is welcomed into his eternal home. You hear the Lord say, "Well done, My good and faithful servant. You have been faithful over a few things, I will make you ruler over many. Come, blessed of My Father, and feast with Me at My table." Your heart bursts with joy, knowing that his example is now being relived by all of his children, grandchildren, and dozens of great-grandchildren for decades to come.

At his funeral, the church fills with friends and family who gather to mourn his loss and celebrate his life. You listen as people share seemingly endless stories with his family, expressing gratefulness for all that Timothy had done and meant to them. They cry with hope, resting in the fact that he will be with his Lord forever and will be remembered on earth for many generations to come.

Inspired by his story and with tears in your eyes, you smile as you deeply consider the awesome vision you have just experienced. And the importance of your own role as a husband and father becomes crystal clear. Every man will truly reap what he sows. You had never understood it quite this clearly before, but now it has become the burning desire of your heart.

Then a horrific thought comes to your mind. You turn to God and ask, "Lord, which one is true? Which account is truly Timothy's end?"

The Lord looks into your eyes, and the smile leaves His face.

"No, God, please don't tell me that everything I've just seen is gone and never happened! Lord, I care about this man and his family now. I beg you, please don't tell me the beauty and rewards of his life are lost, that he's actually the man you showed me at first."

As you look into His eyes, your heart begins to ache with His. "Now you share in the sorrow of what I feel every day," the Lord says, "as I watch men waste their lives."

Your eyes fill with tears as you grieve deeply and weep before the Lord. "But they don't know, God. They don't realize how much is at stake here. They've never seen what it really looks like. They haven't seen the difference, the way You've shown me here tonight."

"But *you* have. And if they will read My Word, they can see it too. Both of these stories are being written right now in the lives of fathers around the world. But what is important now is to resolve which man *you* will become. Will you turn from your sins and completely trust me with your life? Will you take responsibility to be who I have created you to be? Will you obey My Word faithfully until the day of your death? You can resolve to be this kind of man; and you can finish well. Or you can live for yourself and lose so many of the incredible rewards I have placed before you."

"But, Lord," you say, "I didn't have a father like Timothy had. My dad was nothing like James. I've missed out on so much. I was never loved, mentored, and blessed like that by my dad."

"Then you need to use the rest of your life to be the one who breaks the chain and creates a new legacy for your family. You have seen the paths of both. It is now time for you to choose."

> I call heaven and earth to witness against you today, that I have set before you life and death, the blessing and the curse. So choose life in order that you may live, you and your descendants, by loving the LORD your God, by obeying His voice, and by holding fast to Him; for this is your life and the length of your days.
> (Deuteronomy 30:19–20)

COURAGEOUS CHALLENGE

Pray for God to give you His vision for generational faithfulness.

MEMORY VERSE

Therefore, if anyone is in Christ, he is a new creation; old things have passed away; behold, all things have become new. (2 Corinthians 5:17 NKJV)

Do not be like your fathers and your brothers, who were unfaithful to the LORD God of their fathers, so that He made them a horror . . . for if you return to the LORD, your brothers and your sons will find compassion.

2 Chronicles 30:7, 9

CHAPTER 3
BECOMING A CHAIN BREAKER

If anyone is in Christ, he is a new
creation; old things have passed away;
behold, all things have become new.
                              2 Corinthians 5:17 NKJV

As we prepare to dive into the points of
Resolution in future chapters, it's important
to identify one preliminary battleground
that will greatly influence your future success. It's something that applies to all of us
in one way or another. If we do not understand this and learn to walk in victory, our
best intentions at following through on our
other commitments will be very limited.

Here it is: we need to ask God to break
the chains in our lives and from our past.
We need to become *chain breakers* — men
who break away from anything holding us
back from leaving a new legacy of faithfulness behind us. A chain breaker is the fork
in his family tree. He's the one God uses to

end the legacy of rebellion against God that he may have learned from his parents and grandparents. Instead he passes on a legacy of faith, faithfulness, and blessing to his children and grandchildren, giving them a new model of obedience to follow.

The generations of a family will lead one another further and further away from God unless a chain breaker steps up and turns things around — because although children are not punished for the sins of their parents, they are definitely affected and negatively influenced by them. There are no perfect fathers. Like everyone else, they are flawed, sinful, human beings who make mistakes. But because of their spiritual authority and influential position in our lives, they have impacted who we are, what we experience, what we believe, and what direction we've taken as we've grown up. Not only do we receive a sin *nature* from them but sin *nurturing.* We will tend to live in their wake, be influenced by their same mistakes, believe the same lies, and maybe even struggle with their same issues and addictions.

Unless . . .

This powerful "unless" is the liberating message of this chapter. We will go backward *unless* we break free from our family weaknesses by the power of God — by seeking Him, trusting Him, and following Him instead.

But before we go any further, let's clarify that the intent of this chapter is not to blame your parents for your own problems. They may have influenced you, but you are now responsible — not them — for your own sins. The Scriptures repeatedly teach that you should "honor your father and your mother" (Exodus 20:12). You should thank God for them regardless of their example knowing that God is the One who established your family of origin (Psalm 139:13–16). He placed you into their home for a reason. The Bible says:

> The God who made the world and everything in it . . . gives all men life and breath and everything else . . . and he determined the times set for them and the exact places where they should live. God did this so that men would seek him and perhaps reach out for him and find him, though he is not far from each one of us.
> (Acts 17:24–27 NIV)

Did you see that? God "determined the times" set for you and the "exact places" where you would live — *for a reason* — so that you would seek Him and ultimately find Him. No matter the circumstances of your birth, you were not an accident. God knew and allowed your parents to bring you into the world just the way they did and exactly when they did.

Proverbs 20:24 says, "Man's steps are ordained by the LORD. How then can man understand his way?" Though you may not have understood your path, God has been guiding your steps. It's not a mistake that you are who you are and that your parents are (or were) your parents. And the truth is, if you were to know everything God knows, you wouldn't have had it any other way.

So despite any wrongs and pains you have been through, you have been intentionally placed in a position for God to use every one of your experiences for a greater good. To draw you into a relationship with Him. To develop your character and make you more like Jesus. To show how He can overcome any obstacle. To reveal His glory.

If you're willing to view your life from God's providential vantage point, then it's clear you don't have to be crippled by any of the negative aspects in your family tree. You can now see them as paths to avoid, strongholds to conquer, and opportunities to reveal God's power in your life.

You could be the very one God has strategically placed in your family to turn things around. By seeking and finding God in your circumstances and by becoming completely dependent upon Him, you will be changing the game for future generations — starting right now, with your own family. It's time to break some chains!

There are three kinds of chains present in all of our lives:

- Chains that come from *nature* — our inbred sinful nature we received from our parents
- Chains that come from *choices* — sins we commit ourselves and the bondage that follows
- Chains that come from *nurture* — hurtful examples, lies, and worldly traditions we follow

As we discuss chains that may be in your life, we must start by acknowledging that God is the key to the long-term success of you and your family. He is the ultimate Chain Breaker. Jesus launched His ministry by stating how He had been sent "to proclaim release to the captives" and "to set free those who are oppressed" (Luke 4:18). Paul confirmed this when he stated, "O wretched man that I am! Who will deliver me from this body of death? I thank God — through Jesus Christ our Lord!" (Romans 7:24–25 NKJV). Whether it is our inborn sin nature or bad nurturing from a destructive influence, we should realize that surrendering our lives to Jesus Christ *and* living out the victory He has already won through His death on the cross are the foundations for being liberated from every chain. The power to break every curse is resident in His salvation. But let's focus our lens even further and discover specific, biblical truths that will help us live in His freedom. Fasten your seat belt and hang on!

BREAKING THE CHAINS FROM OUR SIN NATURE AND SINFUL CHOICES

We are each born with a bent towards sin. In addition to this, Jesus revealed that when we commit sin, we actually become the "slave of sin" (John 8:34). It becomes our master, and we end up giving ourselves — mind, will, and body — in service to it. We know what that feels like. We know how hard it can be to escape our particular sins, addictions, and wrong habits — especially those modeled to us by our fathers.

But as Jesus explained, He is the key to freedom. "If the Son makes you free," He said, "you will be free indeed." (John 8:36). Our freedom comes in Christ. Jesus has already paid the penalty and completely broken the power and curse of sin through His death on the cross (Colossians 2:13–15; Galatians 3:13). Through faith in Him, we are invited to experience the "surpassing greatness" of His resurrection power (Ephesians 1:19) — yes, the power God used to raise Jesus from the dead — applying that same kind of cleansing force to our most stubborn, ground-in habits.

The apostle Paul explained that if a man's faith is in Christ, he is transformed and his entire spiritual status changes. He becomes "dead" to sin and "alive to God" (Romans 6:11). Sin no longer has the right or authority to "reign" over him and make him "obey" its every whim; instead he is free to live as someone "alive from the dead," using his body for good as an "instrument of righteousness" rather than as a tool of bondage (Romans 6:12–13). But if a man doesn't realize this, he won't tend to believe it, receive it, and walk in it.

So when it comes to dealing with sin — even repeated generational sin — true repentance and faith in Jesus Christ is the solution. A man should first repent and place his faith in Jesus Christ alone to find eternal salvation. But then as a new creation and a believer in Christ, he should continue to repent any time he fails so that he can keep walking in daily victory over sin.

Either way, repentance is a gift from God. It means making a permanent U-turn through a change of mind, a change of heart, and ultimately a change of lifestyle. Repentance happens when you get honest with God about the sins you have committed, and then turn your life in opposition to them — turning to Christ instead so that by the "knowledge of the truth," you can "escape from the snare of the devil" (2 Timothy 2:25–26). *Repentance* means taking God's hand, getting up out of the mud, walking away, and knowing you never have to turn back.

The more we discover who God is, the more we will love, fear, and respect Him. This in turn leads us to understand and desire to live in true repentance, which results in long-term change. Too many men only halfheartedly repent of their sin and then blame God for not being set free. They want freedom from guilt rather than intimacy with their Maker. Instead of "divorcing" themselves from sin, they opt for a "temporary separation" . . . until later. They refuse to live in the victory that the grace of

Christ freely offers them.

But when a man turns humbly and whole-heartedly to Him for help, the Lord can break the bondage of sin in his life completely. (Romans 6–8 explains this.) God's love satisfies where sin could not (John 4:13–14; 1 John 2:15–17).

Then the restlessness from guilt and indecision can end because your conscience is clear and your mind made up. It doesn't mean you won't still be tempted, but you no longer have to be tormented by it. You will still need to continually rely on God's Spirit and power each day to walk in this victory. But the power to win is present, and the roller coaster of bondage can stop. Falling becomes abnormal rather than routine. Freedom becomes a daily reality. Isn't that what we all really want?

So whether the problem starts with sins you learned from your parents or picked up on your own, it's time to repent. To get real, quit hiding your sin in the dark, and walk in the light. To walk by faith in Jesus Christ and surrender to His lordship. To live in and enjoy the victory He has already won for you on the cross. Shine a spotlight on your sins so they can no longer thrive in your heart, your home, or your family.

Your children, of course, will be born with

a sin nature and will also need to place their faith in Christ to walk in freedom. But you don't have to leave them the stumbling block of their father's unfaithfulness and defeat. You can break the chain and leave a new legacy of victory in Christ instead!

BREAKING THE CHAINS OF NURTURE

There are chains forged from nature, chains that result from our choices, and then this third type of chain — which tends to fall into three distinct categories:

Hurtful Examples

You may have had a great dad whom you deeply respect and admire. But if you are like the majority of men, you have vivid memories of sinful examples and hurtful things your father did and said to you over the years. If someone else had done the same thing, it wouldn't have been such a big deal. But because it was your dad, it was devastating.

To him, those moments were likely not as poignant — just passing acts of thoughtlessness or anger that came, went, and were quickly forgotten. But to you, they were monumental, defining moments — poisonous darts that struck your heart, leaving you wounded and confused. You have relived those horrific seconds in your mind count-less times and can still describe in visceral detail the emotions you felt afterwards.

Or you may have been wounded more by your father's *absence* than by his harsh words or abuse. What *you* can describe is the upsetting void of unmet needs and unanswered questions he left hanging in your life.

But regardless, you have been wronged in some way. All of us have. That's not the question. The question is whether or not you will allow it to hinder you or help you. Will you let bitterness tie a chain from your parents' past mistakes to your emotions in the present, limiting your ability to walk in freedom in the future? Because that is what it does. Unforgiveness chains us to the past. Unresolved anger becomes a bitter cancer that poisons hearts. And like all cancers, it must be attacked and eliminated. God wants you to give all of the injustice, hurt, anger, and confusion from your past com-pletely over to Him. To break the chain. *To forgive.* Not just your dad but anyone who has wronged you.

We know the resistance our hearts feel toward the idea. This seems unfair because those who have hurt you do not deserve your forgiveness. But *no one* deserves or earns forgiveness; it must be granted. God's forgiveness of us, for example, is not based upon the fact that we deserve it, but rather upon God's mercy toward us through Christ's spiritual "debt payment" on the cross.

And we are to forgive like God forgives (Ephesians 4:32) — completely, fully, and freely. If we don't forgive, we will constantly allow the past to hinder, hurt, and influence us.

But when we do forgive, it releases the baggage and begins the healing process. It positions you to grow in faith and to become the father you wish you'd had. Unresolved bitterness is sin, and it will distort your own fathering. It will turn you into the very man you don't want to be. But the freedom of letting it all go will result in renewal instead of more grief and hurt.

As long as you hold on to bitterness, you keep yourself in the judge's seat, bearing all the responsibility of making sure those who've offended you get justice. But by choosing to move forward and forgive, not only do you enjoy the fruits of pleasing the Lord, but you trust Him to be the righteous judge He already is, able to pass perfect judgment on anyone who has wronged you. You let it be *His* job, not yours. And then you can go on ahead with life . . . without all the headaches associated with bitterness.

Again, don't hear us saying that forgiveness is an easy thing to do. It is not. It is brave. *Courageous.* But God can give you the grace today to forgive if you first acknowledge your need to do so, and then pray for the desire and ability to let go of your past hurts. But it doesn't have to be complicated. You can dig up the hurt right now, acknowledge it was wrong, and from your heart pray, "Lord, I forgive!" — and then experience breakthrough. It's like taking off the parking brake spiritually. That's the power of forgiveness. To break this bitter chain!

Lies

Jesus said, "If you continue in My word . . . you will know the truth, and the truth will make you free" (John 8:31–32). And since the truth sets us free, we should recognize that lies keep us in bondage. If you believe the same lies your father believed, you will also be bound by them.

Lies about other races, for example, can lead to racism. Lies about God can lead to rebellion and agnosticism. Lies about our origins as human beings and our moral responsibilities can lead to a life of self-hatred, vanity, or destructive hedonism. Lies can cause us to fear and give up, even when there's nothing to be afraid of. If a thief can convince you his toy gun is a loaded weapon, you may tremble and surrender when you don't have to.

But for every angry father who tells his son, "You'll never amount to anything," God the Father says, "I love you dearly and have a higher purpose for your life." For every demeaning name an unwise dad calls his young son, God says, "You are priceless, unique, and special to me." For every lie that says you need to sin, lust, or feed an addiction to survive or be happy, God says, "I will take care of you, will never leave you, and will meet all your needs" (1 Corinthians 10:13; Philippians 4:19).

Despite every lie you've heard, God has a contrasting truth that can liberate you. But the truth doesn't set you free if you only hear it and mentally understand it. You must embrace and believe it in the depths of who you are. You must reject everything that seeks to contradict it, anything that seems on the surface to disprove it, and anyone's opinions that lure you away from believing it. If God is your Father, you can count on the Holy Spirit to open your eyes and illumine His truth. He will burn it into your heart as you read the Bible, ingrain it into your thinking, live it out in obedience, and let Him continually keep you aligned with ultimate reality.

So begin asking God to reveal the lies you have believed in the past and help you replace each one with His truth. As you study God's Word, consider memorizing verses that stand against any lies you have believed. When you discover a lie that's still influencing your thought processes, cast it out and refuse to let it back in, "taking every thought captive to the obedience of Christ" (2 Corinthians 10:5). Break their power not only in your own life but in the lives of your children as you pass God's truth along to them!

Worldly Traditions

Family traditions can be a wonderful way to honor the past and bond families together in celebration. But not all traditions are good. Bad family traditions and twisted cultural philosophies can trap you if you're not careful. The Scripture warns, "See to it that no one takes you captive through philosophy and empty deception, according to the *tradition of men,* according to the elementary principles of the world, rather than according to Christ" (Colossians 2:8).

Just because everyone in your extended family has always believed or done something doesn't make it right for you. Just because it's popular in culture doesn't mean God approves of it or wants you to follow it.

Jesus rebuked some of the people around him by asking them, "Why do you yourselves transgress the commandment of God for the sake of your tradition?" (Matthew 15:3). Some traditions are good, healthy, fun, and conducive to faith-building and lasting memories. Some, on the other hand, are clearly sinful, foolish, and vain. Others add unnecessary burdens to your family.

Some cultural traditions imply that the teenage years should be wasted. Or that it's permissible to be sexually immoral while single. Or that certain holidays are not officially celebrated unless you overeat and drown yourself in alcohol. Some churches *traditionally* reject people from other races. Some families *traditionally* fight about everything. Others expect married children to be more loyal to their parents than to their spouse.

But a man of resolution doesn't keep a tradition alive merely because it's always been that way. He doesn't bow to the status quo or commit things blindly to his calendar without questioning whether it's right before God and good for his family. He doesn't follow along passively just because he's worried what others might think or say.

Chain breakers use Scripture and wisdom to define and filter. They carefully consider which traditions are worth allegiance, discerning which ones honor God and which ones will only tempt and coax them into sinful, wasteful habits.

Many traditions may coincide perfectly with what God's Word has been encouraging all along. But when they don't, a chain breaker marshals the courage to chart a different course, leading his children where he believes their heavenly Father wants them to go. Then he launches new traditions to replace bad ones and creates strong momentum for generations to come!

BREAKING CHAINS THROUGH STRATEGIC PRAYER

Prayer is powerful. It is humbly, honestly, respectfully talking to God. And a chain breaker must learn to become an *intercessor* — a man who shows his true dependence on God by faithfully fighting battles in prayer, both for himself and his family. When a man intercedes — like many great men of the Bible did (Ezra 9:5–15; Nehemiah 9; Jeremiah 14:19–22) — he stands in the gap where evil and problems are rising up against him, and he prays for God to intervene and show mercy instead. Just as Abraham interceded for Lot (Genesis 18:16–33) and Moses interceded for Israel (Numbers 14:11–19), you must become an intercessor who prays on behalf of your marriage, children, and grandchildren.

One praying man can make a major impact. "The effective prayer of a righteous man can accomplish much" (James 5:16). When young King Josiah read God's Word for the first time, he realized that he and his nation would suffer because of the sins of their fathers. So he turned to his priest and servants and said to them, "Go, inquire of the LORD for me and the people and all Judah concerning the words of this book that has been found, for great is the wrath of the LORD that burns against us, because our fathers have not listened to the words of this book, to do according to all that is written concerning us" (2 Kings 22:13).

History tells us that Josiah became a mighty chain breaker. He got busy seeking God and removing anything from the kingdom his father had left him that was dishonoring to the Lord. Because of his intercession, God mightily blessed Josiah and also withheld His wrath during Josiah's reign.

Intercessors break chains. They openly acknowledge sins from the past, then ask God to show mercy to their marriages and children as they realign their purposes with the teachings of His Word. Jeremiah lamented, "Our fathers sinned, and are no more; it is we who have borne their iniquities." Later he prayed, "Restore us to You, O LORD, that we may be restored; renew our days" (Lamentations 5:7, 21). You, too, can ask God right now to begin the process of "delivering" your family from evil and "restoring" them back to Himself. And God — the ultimate Chain Breaker — will not disappoint any man who comes to Him in faith.

CONSISTENCY THROUGH CONSECRATION

When chains are broken, it is important to walk in long-term freedom. One thing that helps us do so is the biblical concept of *consecration,* which means to clean something up and then dedicate it to God. It means cleansing your life and home from any stumbling blocks or evil influences and then presenting yourself and your family into God's hands.

A man makes a powerful declaration when

he says, "God, I dedicate my family and all I have to You. I give you full ownership of my marriage, children, and possessions, and ask You to use us for Your honor!"

As part of your dedication, if there are influences in your home that dishonor God or are pulling you or your family members away from God, you should seriously consider removing them, just as the God-fearing believers in Ephesus did (Acts 19:18–20). Jesus said to remove anything that causes you to sin (Matthew 18:7–9). The writer of Hebrews said to drop any weights that entangle you (Hebrews 12:1–2). Ask God to show you what this may mean for your family. This will set up an ideal environment where His work could take hold and change hearts long-term in the future.

As a father intent on leading your family in the direction of faithfulness to God, you cannot allow entanglements to stand in the way of what God wants to accomplish through you and your new legacy.

In the Old Testament, when King Hezekiah rose to the throne after the death of Ahaz, he repaired God's temple that his wicked father had defamed and desecrated. He then threw out man-made idols and reestablished the worship of God as the centerpiece of his leadership. He said to the priests, "Consecrate yourselves now, and consecrate the house of the LORD, the God of your fathers, and carry the uncleanness out from the holy place. For our fathers have been unfaithful and have done evil in the sight of the LORD our God, and have forsaken Him and turned their faces away from the dwelling place of the LORD, and have turned their backs" (2 Chronicles 29:5–6). Hezekiah made a new commitment to God, declaring that his generation would take things in a different direction — *God's* direction. Then God's blessing followed in mighty ways.

We challenge you to begin the process today of dedicating your family to God in your heart and in action. God blesses and uses what is placed in His hands.

FOR FUTURE GENERATIONS

We are very passionate about the implications of this chapter because our father was the chain breaker. He chose not to follow in the footsteps of his father or grandfather who had both wasted years of their lives in alcoholism, immorality, and rebellion against God. Instead our father surrendered his life to Jesus Christ, forgave his father for all the pain he had brought on him, and then allowed the Word of God to teach him how to be a godly husband and father.

He married a wonderful, godly woman and dedicated each of us as his children to the Lord. Because of this, we grew up in a strong, loving home, living in the rewards and blessings that follow a godly man of integrity (Psalm 112). We didn't stumble upon our dad looking at pornography; instead we found him on his knees interceding on behalf of his family and children. We are so grateful that God's grace and truth penetrated into our dad's heart and he responded with faith, courage, and obedience. This has made a huge difference for all three of his sons now and his fifteen grandchildren.

As a chain breaker, you too can turn the calendar page from yesterday to today, building on what's golden and godly from your past, yet hauling off whatever has cluttered your life with sinful attachments. Then moving forward in your resolve for godly manhood, you must often make some difficult, deliberate decisions:

- Where sin has crept into your life — *repent*
- Where bitterness has taken root in your heart — *forgive*

- Where lies have been woven into the script — *seek truth*
- Where traditions have taken precedence — *start fresh*
- Where problems have tried to steal and malign — *pray*
- Where hindrances are piling up — *consecrate and dedicate your family to God*

These are the kinds of ongoing principles that will prove the difference between *signing* a resolution and becoming a *man* of resolution. God wants you to seek Him and find Him so you can know Him and love Him. His intent from the beginning has always been to use you for His glory. And there is nothing greater, more fulfilling, or more important than living with this goal in mind.

This is why it is so important to free yourself of any weights, burdens, or chains that would prevent you and your family from running the race of life to your fullest potential for God's glory. He can break any chain from your past and allow you to inspire a legacy of faithfulness for future generations.

So it's time to move forward. To grow in faith and strength. To take back surrendered ground. To form a bold, protective blockade of blessing for future generations. Let's start where we are and go forward as fast as we can. From God's heart to our reality.

By His grace, we can become faithful men of resolution.

COURAGEOUS CHALLENGE

Consecrate your family by praying and dedicating them to God.

MEMORY VERSE

Jesus said, "If you hold to my teaching, you are really my disciples. Then you will know the truth, and the truth will set you free." (John 8:31–32 NIV)

■ ■ ■ ■

PART TWO:
COMMITTING TO
THE RESOLUTION

■ ■ ■ ■

When I was a child, I used to speak like a child, think like a child, reason like a child; when I became a man, I did away with childish things.

1 Corinthians 13:11

CHAPTER 4
RESOLVE TO BE A
MAN OF RESPONSIBILITY

I DO solemnly resolve before God to take full responsibility for myself, my wife, and my children.

When did you become a man? Can you answer that question? Was it when you started driving a car or took your first job? Was it when you left home? Some wonder if it was when they were married, had sex the first time; others when they could legally vote or fight for their country. Men are often unsure.

We have a generation of men today in their thirties still wondering if they have truly become men yet. And if they were told that they were indeed one, they wouldn't really know what that means. This frustration is common in our gender-confused culture, which leaves men with more questions than authoritative answers.

But God's Word gives us clear insight as

to when a boy steps into manhood and what it means to be a man. Learning this can not only help us understand ourselves better but also help our sons become secure men as well.

Growing into manhood is a process that takes place between two bookends. Puberty is the obvious starting point God has established biologically to mark the first stage of manhood. When Jesus was twelve years old and His parents accidentally left Him in Jerusalem after the Passover, His response to being alone communicated that He had already started stepping into manhood. After they went back to look for Him, they didn't find Him in a back alley playing with children. They found Him in the temple already embracing the things of men, "sitting in the midst of the teachers, both listening to them and asking them questions. And all who heard Him were amazed at His understanding and His answers" (Luke 2:46–47).

His worried mother, still considering him a boy, said, "Son, why have You done this to us? Look, Your father and I have sought You anxiously." But Jesus said to them, "Why did you seek Me? Did you not know that I must be about My Father's business?" (Luke 2:48–49 NKJV).

Though Jesus was likely just entering puberty, His mental, social, and spiritual development into manhood had already begun. For after this event, the Scriptures say that He "kept increasing in wisdom and stature, and in favor with God and men" (Luke 2:52). He kept maturing in His thinking *mentally,* in His body *physically,* in His fellowship with God *spiritually,* and in His relationships with others *socially.*

He was becoming a man.

In the Jewish community today, when a boy reaches puberty (around the age of thirteen), the Bar Mitzvah ceremony signals his exodus from childhood and the beginning of his manhood. The Hebrew word *Bar* means "son of." *Mitzvah* means "the law" or "the commandment." During a Bar Mitzvah ceremony, the boy's father and other trusted men call him into manhood, embrace him, and allow him to read aloud from the Old Testament Scriptures. He is now to learn and obey the commands of God on his own as a "son of the law," and his parents now consider him accountable for his own sins. After this event he is considered mature enough to own property and be married in the future when he is ready. He understands he must now embrace responsibility for his own life, start stepping into his manhood and acting like a man. This rite of passage makes the experience of becoming a man clear to everyone involved.

The Bible also reveals the other bookend marking full arrival into manhood. If puberty is where manhood begins, many passages indicate that by *twenty* years of age, a male is considered an adult man in the eyes of God.

- When the Old Testament Israelites were asked to give a financial contribution during a census, God required it of every man "twenty years old and over." (Exodus 30:14)
- When they made vows to help fund the sanctuary, God stated that men must give the most — identifying them as any "male from twenty years even to sixty years old." (Leviticus 27:3)
- The individuals God acknowledged as ready to fight in war for Israel were men who were "twenty years old and upward." (Numbers 1:3)
- And when Israel sinned and grumbled against the Lord, the men who were held accountable and punished severely by God were, again, those "twenty years old and upward."

(Numbers 14:29)

So in God's eyes, every lesson and preparation that was required in order for a boy to become a fully accountable, responsible man was expected to happen during this roughly seven-year window between puberty and the age of twenty. He may have become a responsible adult earlier than twenty, but by then he had no excuse. This expectation of responsibility should guide and influence our thinking today.

This means, then, that the first *Resolution* point — if you're twenty or older — has something very important for you to embrace.

I do solemnly resolve before God to take full responsibility for myself, my wife, and my children

Whether you are currently married or not, or have children or not, you're a man. And as a man, God calls you to an appropriate and excellent standard: *His.*

A standard of initiative, self-control, and eager acceptance of your vital roles.

A high level of expectation for certain attributes to become part of the fiber of your being.

To be a man is to fully own your roles as an adult, husband, father, employee, neighbor, and any other role you choose to undertake. But what does taking responsibility for your manhood look like? How do you recognize it in yourself? What are you supposed to be shooting for, and how does God help you overcome the obstacles that exist between where you are and where He wants you to be?

In this chapter, we'd like to show you seven attributes indicated in Scripture that define what true manhood is and should be. These things should be developing in every boy as he becomes a man. And every man, regardless of age, needs to find these within himself and be living them out. Here they are . . .

1. A MAN ACCEPTS HIS MASCULINITY

Masculinity is generally understood as having the characteristics of maleness. But the key ingredient is actually *strength*. From childhood, God has put a longing inside us to be strong. A boy doesn't twirl in front of the mirror; he flexes his muscles instead. The natural competitiveness and aggressiveness in men is often a testing and demonstration of their strength. But like Jesus, every man also needs to be developing moral, mental, social, and spiritual strength. That's because all of our key roles in life will require greater strength in order to carry them out.

If men do not develop a sense of their own fortitude, they will never attempt hard things, lead their families, fight for their country, or confront evil. Instead they will become irresponsible, passive cowards who are easily swayed and give up when the pressure is on. The apostle John wrote, "I have written to you, young men, because you are strong, and the word of God abides in you, and you have overcome the evil one" (1 John 2:14).

The opposite of masculinity is to be feminine, which means soft, pretty, and delicate. It is the perfect complement to masculinity. God intentionally made women weaker in some ways so that men would view them like fine china or fragile jewelry. Not as possessions, but as being extremely valuable. Always treated with honor and tender care.

The apostle Peter wrote, "You husbands in the same way, live with your wives in an understanding way, as with someone weaker, since she is a woman; and show her honor" (1 Peter 3:7). He didn't say women are weak, but "weaker" in comparison to men. It's ironic that our feminist indoctrinated culture has spent decades telling women to "Rise up and be strong!" and telling men to "Sit down and be quiet!"

Despite this, it is a father's job to call his sons into manhood. He should challenge them to embrace their masculinity, be like Jesus, and become mentally, physically, spiritually, and socially strong. To walk, talk, and act like a strong man. King David charged his son Solomon, "Be strong, therefore, and show yourself a man" (1 Kings 2:2).

So if you are an adult male, twenty years of age or older, then God considers you a man! But if you are going to obey Him and be faithful to Him until the end, you must act like a man, embrace your masculinity, and hear His command to "Be strong!" (Joshua 1:9).

Then as a man, when times get rough, you must not quit. When everything seems against you, you cannot run away. When you fall or fail — as all of us do — you must own your mistakes, get back on your feet, and not shirk your responsibilities. When the enemy is attacking, you must keep up your resistance — "and having done everything, to stand firm" (Ephesians 6:13). You must keep doing the right thing and fighting for what is true and noble. You must obey God's Word that says to all of us, "Act like men, be strong!" (1 Corinthians 16:13). This is our responsibility as men. This is required of us to be faithful.

2. A MAN SPEAKS AND ACTS WITH MATURITY

The apostle Paul said, "When I was a child, I used to speak like a child, think like a child, reason like a child; when I became a man, I did away with childish things" (1 Corinthians 13:11). A vital transition must take place as a boy becomes a man. He must intentionally choose to let go of childishness and foolishness.

Clinging to childhood while growing into manhood is like trying to run in opposite directions at the same time. The "Peter Pan Syndrome" is a modern term often used to describe immature men who refuse to grow up.

Because teen years are often wasted and fathers have become silent, this generation of young men doesn't know why they are here or what God has called them to become. So they wander into the future, drown themselves in entertainment, and live for the weekend rather than for eternity. Rather than being responsible men of their word, they are noncommittal and dependent upon their mothers. Rather than excelling and leading like previous generations, they are passively watching women their age surpass them in the classroom and in the marketplace. Rather than initiating serious conversations with wiser men, they goof off with fools in sports bars. Their identities are wrapped up in pleasing themselves and wasting their time, not bettering society and training up the next generation.

They then carry this over into their families. Sometimes it's a thirty-year-old man who won't stop playing video games to read to his children. Or a forty-year-old dad who won't talk with his hurting teenage daughter because it would take time away from a playoff game. Or a father who won't go to church with his family because he stayed up too late watching television shows that only reinforce his immaturity.

Too many men want the freedoms, rewards, and privileges of manhood but only the responsibilities of boyhood. They want intimacy with their wives without loving them as God instructed. They want to be respected by their kids without investing time and discipline in them. They want a higher status at work without raising their own level of honor and integrity.

But if we want to be men, we must resolve that "we will no longer be immature like children. We won't be tossed and blown about by every wind of new teaching. . . . Instead, we will speak the truth in love, growing in every way more and more like Christ" (Ephesians 4:14–15 NLT). We will think the thoughts and speak the words of mature men, not teenage boys. As Paul challenged the early believers, "Do not be children in your thinking. Be infants in evil, but in your thinking be mature" (1 Corinthians 14:20 ESV).

Every man needs to identify and release any leftover childishness from his past. Childhood has come and gone. It's time to repent of wanting to remain there, learn to act our age, and move on to the greater, better, and nobler things of men. "The noble man makes noble plans, and by noble deeds he stands" (Isaiah 32:8 NIV).

3. A MAN EMBRACES RESPONSIBILITY

Men are happiest and at their best when they are responsible — and at their worst when they are not. If you were to boil every point of the *Resolution* down to one statement, it could be this: *We must resolve to fully embrace all of our responsibilities before God.*

The main concept of responsibility is that you are being entrusted and empowered by a higher authority to care for something or someone. And along with this empowerment comes the blessings of doing it well or the consequences of doing it poorly.

The first thing God did after creating the first man, Adam, was to give him responsibilities. He placed him in the garden "to cultivate it and keep it" (Genesis 2:15). This meant he was to work it so that everything under his care would bloom and stay protected. In tandem with this responsibility, God gave Adam increased value, freedom, and the ability to enjoy the fruit of his labor. And just like Adam, we too are wired and empowered by God to accept responsibility into our lives. We each must get busy *cultivating* and *protecting* everything within our jurisdiction. Sin makes men tend to resist responsibility, but embracing it is part of our manhood.

Alex and Brett Harris, authors (at age nineteen) of *Do Hard Things,* tell how history abounds with examples of young men who rose to the occasion after being given great responsibilities. At twelve, David Farragut, the U.S. Navy's first admiral, took command of his first ship by sailing a captured vessel back to America. George

Washington began mastering geometry, trigonometry, and surveying at the same age as a modern fifth or sixth grader. At sixteen he became a county surveyor. At twenty-one he owned 2,300 acres of land.[6]

The reason such stories astound us, the Harris brothers say, is because we view young people through a lens that didn't exist back then — *adolescence* — a relatively modern invention that establishes teen years as a moratorium on responsibility and prolongs childhood indefinitely.

When a young man is passive and irresponsible, he greatly limits his freedoms, opportunities, and successes. Whereas responsibility builds up a man and everything around him, the lack of it only weakens and destroys. Irresponsible men are dangerous to whatever they touch.

For example, whether he is married or not, every man is responsible for his seed. When he isn't, he leaves neglected children behind to struggle with unmet needs and anger, and then to carry on his destructive behavior. When he supports an abortion to escape fatherhood, his selfish avoidance of responsibility is what drives it.

Responsibility calls us to action and tests us. It reveals our character, our caliber, and our commitment. It is both a gift and an honor. And the more maturity a man has, the more responsibility God can trust him with.

So we challenge you to gratefully accept the duties God has given you. Take the steering wheel back into your hands as you guide, protect, and provide for your family. Don't force your wife or children to shoulder what rightfully is on you. While you live and breathe, resolve to bloom and protect everything under your care.

Embrace responsibility! Love it. Live it. Teach it to your children. Model it at home and at work. Initiate it with other men around you. Be the man who makes the call and takes the heat. Come up with the plan and make sure it gets done. Own your mistakes and clean up your own mess. Beg God for wisdom and the guidance to do it well, and then trust Him for the courage never to run from it. "A faithful, sensible servant is one to whom the master can give the responsibility of managing his other household servants and feeding them. If the master returns and finds that the servant has done a good job, there will be a reward" (Luke 12:42–43 NLT).

4. A MAN FUNCTIONS INDEPENDENTLY

Both the Old and New Testaments say that "a man shall leave his father and his mother and be joined to his wife" (Genesis 2:24; Matthew 19:5). Even if a man never marries, God created him to be able to leave home and stand on his own two feet. He should be capable enough to work, function, and live without dependence on anyone else financially, spiritually, or physically.

Though God desires that we not be alone in life, and though we need one another in the body of Christ, a grown man should not need his parents or others taking care of him. He should be a fountain, not a drain. He should seek counsel but function autonomously.

God often uses mothers during our childhood, and our wives in marriage, to point out areas where we are not being responsible or stepping into manhood. They can help us with reminders on the front end, but we should never become dependent upon their "mothering." Like Jesus, the older and more mature a young man gets, the more he will have to pull away from his mother, cut the umbilical cord, and make decisions for himself (Luke 2:48–50; John 2:1–8; Matthew 12:46–50).

So if your mother (or father) is still trying

to run your life, you need to lovingly tell them that you are trying to be the man God has called you to be — that they should *pray* for you but give you (and your wife) the space to make your own decisions. You will never become a responsible man if you allow your parents to control or dominate you during adulthood.

You need your wife's help. But if she is constantly nagging you, then you should learn to outpace her concerns. When she brings up things, you need to already be on it. "I've already taken care of that" should be often flowing from your lips. Anticipate and initiate.

Responsible men are like Christ, who did not let his mother, disciples, or others determine His thoughts, attitudes, or actions. He was completely plugged into the Father, the Holy Spirit, and the Word of God. That's why He was able to be more like a thermostat, affecting His circumstances, rather than like a thermometer, merely reacting to His surroundings. If it hasn't already happened, it's time to cut the cord. Declare — and live — your independence as a man who has taken full responsibility for himself.

5. A Man Can Lead a Family Faithfully

Like the apostle Paul, not all men are called to be married or have children. Singleness can be as much of a "gift from God" as marriage (1 Corinthians 7:7). But as a grown man, Paul was mature and competent enough to marry if he had so chosen (1 Corinthians 9:5). Having the responsibility necessary to start and faithfully lead a family is a clear attribute of manhood.

Manhood does not mean you *should* marry, but you should be able to. There is nothing wrong with waiting to get married, but many men delay it for decades because they are so immature. Then they begin preparing for marriage after they propose. That's like starting to train for the Olympics during the opening ceremonies.

If you are a single man, you should already be learning and locking down the character qualities necessary for marriage and parenting in your heart right now. And if you're already married, it's time to live them out on a daily, diligent basis.

Furthermore, if you are raising a son, you should be teaching him — by your words and actions — the roles and responsibilities of a husband and father. Show him how to love and provide for a woman, as well as how to train and lead his children. Pursue with him the goal that by the time he reaches twenty, he will already be mature enough to get married if he chooses. Then whenever he does, he will readily assume his position as leader, a man who will protect and provide for his family in every necessary way. He won't be flying blind or needing you to handle everything for him. He will be a man. Ready to step up to the plate and hit the long ball. And he will join you in considering it his privilege to lead his family well.

6. A MAN RECOGNIZES HIS ACCOUNTABILITY

All of life's privileges, blessings, and freedoms that come with responsibility also come with a counterweight called *accountability.* Having no accountability always leads to irresponsibility. But Jesus explained that we will each stand before God one day and be held accountable for how we lived. Our actions not only have immediate consequences but eternal ones as well.

"For we will all stand before the judgment seat of God" (Romans 14:10) where He will "judge men's secrets" (Romans 2:16) and "bring to light the things hidden in the darkness," disclosing the motives of our

114

hearts (1 Corinthians 4:5), judging the words of our mouths (Matthew 12:36), and testing the deeds we have done (Romans 2:5–8).

The judgment seat of Christ is not a theory designed to motivate us. It is a reality established by God, wired into our consciences, and confirmed throughout His Word.

Everything in a man's thinking changes when he realizes that he is only one heartbeat away from having to stand before God and give an account for his life. "It is appointed for men to die once," the Bible says, "but after this the judgment" (Hebrews 9:27 NKJV).

The first thing this awakens in him is a question about his spiritual readiness for that coming day. Are you ready to meet God? If you were to be honest, would you say that you know for certain where you will spend eternity after you die? Most men don't understand what God requires for someone to be ready. (If you are not certain and would like an explanation of how to have peace with God and find assurance of going to heaven, see page 377 in the appendix.)

But if you already have a personal relationship with Jesus Christ and are confident that you will spend eternity with Him, remember that you are still accountable as a man for making the most of the rest of your life. We still must take full responsibility for ourselves, our wives, and our children. We must seek and discover God's will. We are responsible for obeying the commands of Christ. This is what we will be held accountable for.

And preparing for that day is why we should become accountable to one another. We should surround ourselves with godly men who will help us prepare to be found faithful. Men who have permission to ask us the tough questions, keep tabs on our spiritual condition, and speak the truth into our lives, even when we don't want to hear it. We need to be reading the Scripture daily, studying it deeply, and obeying it willingly as an ongoing lifestyle. (For help in starting, leading, or participating in a men's *Resolution* group, see page 395).

At the end of his days, King Solomon summarized all the lessons and wisdom of his life with this: "Now all has been heard; here is the conclusion of the matter: Fear God and keep his commandments, for this is the whole duty of man. For God will bring every deed into judgment, including every hidden thing, whether it is good or

evil" (Ecclesiastes 12:13–14 NIV). Accountability dynamically helps make us into men
— humble, wise, responsible, faithful men.

7. A MAN IS AN IMAGE BEARER OF GOD

After creating the earth, plants, and animals,
God (eternally existing as Father, Son, and
Holy Spirit) said, "Let Us make man in Our
image, according to Our likeness" (Genesis
1:26). He specifically formed man in such a
way that He sees His very likeness in us.
What an honor and mysterious privilege!

For although men and women are clearly
equal before God (Galatians 3:28) — neither of them more valuable to Him than the
other — the Scriptures do indicate a difference in the unique way a man bears God's
image and brings Him glory that is a part
of his manhood. A man "is the image and
glory of God; but the woman is the glory of
man" (1 Corinthians 11:7).

According to Genesis 2:23, the word
"woman" means "taken out of man." Because of the way Eve was formed from a
part of Adam to become a complementary
helpmeet for him, God has given wives an
amazing ability to recognize, reveal, and
reflect the character of their husbands. As a
wife reflects God's glory and image herself,

she does so as one under her husband's authority. He in turn is not to bring glory to *himself* — as if he mattered more or had greater intrinsic worth than she does — but to use all his power, authority, and ability to reveal and reflect all glory back to God through his life. Unlike the animals, we uniquely bear our Maker's image. And therefore, in all our choices, words, and behaviors, we need to represent Him well. This is humbling, but it is also our privileged responsibility!

A DEFINITION OF MANHOOD

These seven principles come together to form a single definition of manhood that we hope will help you (and your sons) live as men to the glory of God in the days ahead.

A man is an adult male	*Leviticus 27:3*
who accepts his masculinity	*1 Corinthians 16:13*
speaks and acts with maturity	*1 Corinthians 13:11*
embraces responsibility	*Genesis 1:26; 2:15*

functions independently	Genesis 2:24; Matthew 12:46–50
can lead a family faithfully	Genesis 2:24; 1 Timothy 3:4–5
and recognizes his accountability	Ecclesiastes 12:13–14
as an image bearer of God	Genesis 1:26; 1 Corinthians 11:7–9

These seven attributes need to be developing in every young man during his teenage years. And these are the attributes we should be embracing as grown men, too, for there is eternal significance behind each of them. God wants men to be strong spiritually, mature spiritually, and able to lead and care for others spiritually in the family of God. Living as responsible men on a physical level prepares us to be faithful men on a spiritual level, where it matters most.

So if you haven't been serious or deliberate about it before, it's time! Accept your masculinity, being "strong in the Lord and in the strength of His might" (Ephesians 6:10).

Put away childishness, embrace your own responsibilities, and be faithful to everything that is under your care. Seek your parents' counsel, but don't think you cannot live without their help and approval. Lead your family with courage, and live every day bearing God's image and bringing Him honor, knowing you will one day be held accountable before Him. This is not just our call as men of resolution; this is our call as men.

If you're like most of us, you may feel overwhelmed by a deep sense of inadequacy. But actually, this is right where God wants you. He knows that on our own, none of us has what it takes to be consistently responsible. We will fail miserably without His help. He never compromises the standards, but He calls us to our knees so He can help us live up to them by the power of Christ. We must surrender ourselves to Him and learn to rely daily on His wisdom, strength, and grace. And when we fall short, He offers us truckloads of mercy as we confess it to Him.

By His grace, we don't have to live in failure. We can do all things through Christ who strengthens us! This is how we live as men. This is how responsibility becomes victory!

How blessed is everyone who fears the Lord, who walks in His ways. When you

shall eat of the fruit of your hands, you will be happy and it will be well with you. Your wife shall be like a fruitful vine within your house, your children like olive plants around your table. Behold, for thus shall the man be blessed who fears the Lord.
(Psalm 128:1–4)

COURAGEOUS CHALLENGE

Identify and initiate this week at least one important conversation you need to have with your son(s).

MEMORY VERSE

Be on the alert, stand firm in the faith, act like men, be strong. (1 Corinthians 16:13)

As for me and my house, we will serve the LORD.

Joshua 24:15

CHAPTER 5
RESOLVE TO LEAD
YOUR FAMILY

I WILL love them, protect them, serve
them, and teach them the Word of God
as the spiritual leader of my home.

Moses was dead. And the entire nation of
Israel was in shock. This holy, powerful sage
had led them forty years since their miracu-
lous departure from Egypt. Now he was
gone, and a massive group of people was
stuck precariously in the wilderness and in
desperate need of new leadership.

God turned to Joshua and told him it was
now his job to lead.

Imagine how afraid and unprepared he
must have felt for this task. No one could
be a leader like Moses. Yet in Joshua chapter
1, God laid out a clear leadership path that
would set Joshua up for incredible success.
He promised him four spiritual resources to
help him lead — four resources that are also
available to God's children today in the

leadership of our homes.

- He gave him God-ordained AU-THORITY to "cross this Jordan, you and all this people, to the land which I am giving to them" (Joshua 1:3).
- He gave him God's WORD to meditate upon "day and night," to make his way "prosperous" and his every endeavor a "success" (Joshua 1:8).
- He gave him God's PRESENCE as a reliable companion, guide, and shield. "The LORD your God is with you wherever you go" (Joshua 1:9).
- He gave him God's PEOPLE to support and encourage him (Joshua 1:16–18).

And *seven times* in the midst of his charge to leadership, God encouraged Joshua with the same defining challenge. He repeated the key characteristics that would hold his mantle of leadership together. Again and again Joshua heard: *"Be strong and courageous!"*

This was his leadership model and code. His rallying cry.

Why did God want Joshua to hear these words so many times? Because He knew that a leader tends to become overwhelmed, afraid, and passive. He knew that strength and courage are fundamental ingredients to becoming the leader a man should be.

Leaders are not leaders because they're smarter, more talented, or more organized than those around them. Nor because they're tall or wealthy or more muscular.

Leaders are the ones who take *courage.* Regardless of what is going on around them, they repeatedly exercise the courage to step up and use their influence to move others in the right direction. People will follow a leader even if he doesn't have it all together. But they won't follow a man without courage, because a man without courage won't lead.

The Devil himself will tell you that you don't have what it takes to lead your marriage or your family. He will point out your mistakes and failures of the past. He will play up your lack of understanding and your uncertainty about the future. He will highlight your feelings of fear and inadequacy. And he will convince you to take the easy way — to disengage and become passive, to let somebody else handle it this time. And next time.

But leadership is not about expertise or perfection or public opinion; it's about *courage* — the courage to trust God, to do the right thing, to stand alone, to maintain forward momentum, not to cave under pressure, to get back up after being knocked down, again and again and again.

Yes, leaders should pray. They should ask questions, seek counsel, and rally support. They should rely on God's authority, God's Word, God's presence, and God's people. But at the same time, they must repeatedly keep choosing to be strong and take courage, to take responsibility and keep leading.

And that's what God has called you to do. Starting at home.

YOUR MARRIAGE IS YOUR RESPONSIBILITY

Do you realize that as the leader of your home, the greater responsibility for the success of your marriage is on you? You are driving. When a marriage falls apart, the wife may be responsible, but the husband is more responsible. And he must take the primary blame for any failure because ultimately he is the leader, and he let it happen under his watch.

Too many men are like Adam after he sinned in the Garden of Eden, blaming their wives instead of taking responsibility.

Very, very rarely will a wife want out of a marriage if her husband is leading her well and loving her unconditionally. Even though some women foolishly tear down their marriages with their own hands (Proverbs 14:1), most problems come from husbands not grabbing the wheel and intentionally steering their marriage with vision, love, wisdom, and direction.

All too often, men simply give up when a marriage turns south, or they disengage and sit around waiting for their wives to get their act together. But that's not leadership. *We* are the leaders! We must take courage and always be willing to make the first move, get our own lives in order, then lead our wives by our loving example.

God has put something into men that longs to be courageous. And when a man uses that courage to lead his wife well, she tends to bloom. She respects him more and experiences a greater sense of security. She'll want to follow his lead, and she will feel safe in doing so. But when a wife lives with a leadership void, she will feel constantly pulled into the position of filling it. As she leads her husband, not only does her respect for him weaken, he tends to cower and become even more passive over time. She can be brilliant and strong, but both of them will feel resentment toward each other and less secure together.

Nobody wins. Everybody loses.

The idea of 50/50 leadership is a farce that creates two heads and two people trying to drive at the same time. That's why we can say that when the Bible establishes men as the leaders of their homes, it is in no way a devaluation of women. Our leadership is intended to bless and honor our wives in the highest possible way. When we do so, it brings them great joy and confidence in who they are and helps them exercise their God-given skills, grace, and beauty with generous freedom. Our wives should have the freedom to influence without having to bear the weight of responsibility and accountability that rests on the shoulders of the leader.

Obviously history is littered with self-centered men who have dominated, belittled, ignored, and abused their wives in the name of male leadership. Patriarchal cultures have been notorious for treating women as second-class citizens. And because men are generally taller, physically stronger, and more aggressive than women, they have often become the bullies on the playground, the tyrants in government — the insensitive egotists in their homes. This is incredibly wrong on multiple levels and has never been God's will or intent.

Let's make that clear.

In the world, the strong take advantage of and abuse the weak, using them for their own personal pleasure or advantage at the other's expense. But in God's biblical design of leadership, the strong die for the weak. Those in charge lay down their lives for the ones under their care. The leader serves and protects. The more powerful or influential you are, the more humble, servant-hearted, and sacrificial you are to become.

That's God's way.

And should be *our* way.

Think about it. Jesus, God's Son — the most powerful leader of all time — had the authority to cast out demons, heal the sick, raise the dead, and calm violent storms. But when it came to those under His authority, He served and shepherded them instead of throwing His weight around. He cared for their needs and then willingly died for them by His own volition. Instead of trampling them under His feet, He knelt down and *washed* their feet. Jesus explained God's leadership design this way:

You know that the rulers in this world lord it over their people, and officials flaunt their authority over those under them. But among you it will be different. Whoever wants to be a leader among you must be your servant, and whoever wants to be first among you must be the slave of everyone else. For even the Son of Man came not to be served but to serve others and to give his life as a ransom for many. (Mark 10:42–45 NLT)

That's courage.

And it works beautifully in marriage.

When God places the husband in leadership over his wife, He gives her the title of Beloved and commands her husband to love her unconditionally like Jesus loved the church. He should cherish her, nourish her, and lay down his life for her. No other culture, political group, or system of belief comes even close to that level of sacrificial honor and proper respect for women. For there is no "greater love" than that (John 15:13).

As the husband, give your wife the strong protection and provision she needs. Free her up from carrying the marriage and family. Rescue her. And give her the time to pour life, love, and attention into your children.

God's Word says you are to live with her "in an understanding way" (1 Peter 3:7), serving her the way Jesus modeled for us. Treat her with honor as a "fellow heir of the grace of life," or else God says your prayer life will be "hindered." You will always need her counsel, discernment, and support to be successful in your role, but don't let anything keep you from bearing the greatest burden of responsibility in your home. She is called your *helper,* just as God is a "helper" to us (Psalm 54:4), just as the Holy Spirit is a "Helper" who stays with us forever (John 14:16). But she will be a better helper to *you* when you help *her,* when you bear the greater load. Women are perfectly designed to partner with us so that our strengths complement one another's weaknesses, so that together we glorify God more fully within the context of mutual respect and unconditional love.

So lead your wife by serving her well.

But don't let your courage end there.

YOUR CHILDREN ARE YOUR RESPONSIBILITY

Let's take it a step further. As the God-ordained leader of your home, the primary responsibility for the training and rearing of children is *also* on the shoulders of their father. This is not your wife's sole job, or the school system's, or even the church's.

It's on *you* as the dad. This doesn't mean your wife is not an active part of the process, but it does mean the greater responsibility is yours.

Both the Old and New Testaments commission dads specifically to train up their kids and lead them toward spiritual maturity and success in life. Moses told the men in leadership over Israel to teach their children — "when you sit in your house and when you walk by the way and when you lie down and when you rise up" (Deuteronomy 6:7) — so that they and their grandchildren would learn to love, fear, and obey God. Later, in the New Testament, when the issue of child rearing came up in the early church, Paul directed his message specifically to men, saying, "Fathers, do not provoke your children to anger, but bring them up in the discipline and instruction of the Lord" (Ephesians 6:4).

Sadly the majority of kids today are forsaking their church and faith after they graduate from high school. This is primarily the result of poor fathering. When dads lead spiritually, studies suggest that kids are up to *twenty times* more likely to stay in church long-term than when moms are the spiritual leaders at home.[7]

If your kids are floundering, rebelling, or

falling apart, there may be many reasons it's happening. But the bottom line is, it is happening under your watch. And though you cannot control everything or fix it all overnight, you can be courageous enough to reengage with their issues now and make whatever changes necessary to turn things around with God's ever-present help.

A good leader doesn't waste his time playing the blame game. Instead he gets immediately involved, leading with purpose, dealing with problems, then doing everything possible to prevent them from happening again. Even if your kids are grown and gone, it's never too late to reach out to them and become a positive influence in their lives by praying, encouraging, counseling, and cheering them on. Until a man dies, his powerful position as a father and a grandfather still lives on. His remaining chapters are still to be written.

In saying all of this, we're not trying to load you down with guilt or to make what already seems like an impossible job even harder. Again, we understand that even such major problems as divorce or a child's rebellion are not always a man's fault. There are so many things involved by the time a situation gets this serious, and sometimes the issues are bigger than your love and leadership can completely control. But the likelihood of trouble skyrockets when a man becomes passive or disconnected or allows a relational or directional vacuum to develop in his home. And we don't want that happening to you — or to us — by failing to keep God's principles front and center. Our goal is to help you step up and win in the long run.

So this is what we are challenging you to do. Starting today, the phrase "Not on my watch!" needs to be permanently ingrained into your mind-set. It's time to start where you are and go forward as fast as you can. Take full responsibility as the leader of your family.

Be strong and courageous.

But how? Practically speaking.

As the leader in your home, you are called by God to nurture your family with love, protection, and service. But first, with spiritual guidance.

BEING THE SPIRITUAL LEADER

When you break it all down and track it all back, the key to any man's success — as a husband, a father, and everything else — is his own personal walk with God. Not just on Sundays but *every* day. Jesus explained that remaining in close fellowship with God is the secret to true fruitfulness and effectiveness in life (John 15:4–5).

Trusting Him makes you wise. Relying on Him keeps you strong. Following Him shows you how to lead. But He said that if you don't walk with Him, you won't really accomplish anything. Life and relationships are simply too complex and difficult for you to make it on your own reasoning or strength.

So your leadership of your family starts with your own one-on-one time with God. It is so important for a man to set apart time each day for prayer, reading the Scriptures, and tuning his heart with God's heart. This may be a new concept to you, but this is a crucial step and is fundamental to strong spiritual leadership. You may need to rearrange your activities or reduce your entertainment options to do this, but this is foundational and is always worth it.

God loves when men seek Him. "You will seek Me and find Me," He promises, "when you search for Me with all your heart" (Jeremiah 29:13). So choose a time to daily meet with God. Guard it and spend it well.

Seeking God in a very deliberate, devoted manner will impact everything else in your world. By filling your tank with His wisdom and love, He will increasingly enable you to navigate through any storms and help you pour into the lives of your family.

As you focus on your relationship with God, you will find it more natural to want your wife and children to be enjoying the same thing. Jesus uses the Word of God to wash us and bloom us into a holy Bride (John 15:3; Ephesians 5:26). Leading your family with God's Word is a key to helping them work through issues, love one another, and grow spiritually.

Many men are learning how powerful and effective it can be to have a family time of devotion together. Even if it seems awkward or different at first, consider making this a part of your schedule each week. *Be courageous about it!* It's really very easy. You don't have to prepare anything or make it complicated. It can be as simple as getting together in the same room and talking about how everyone is doing, reading a chapter out loud from the Bible, followed by a simple prayer asking God to help you apply what you heard. Try it for one week, and see if you don't find it one of the most bonding and fulfilling aspects of your day.

The more time you spend with your family in God's Word, the more you and your children will discover liberating truths and powerful principles to apply to your lives.

Additionally, the more committed you are to worshipping weekly with your spiritual family at church, the more your children will see this as a priority and want to keep growing and maturing as a follower of Christ. You're not just a leader. You're the key influencer they need as a *spiritual* leader.

And as impossible as that may sound, you can do this. And you can succeed at it. Plug in personally, and then lead the way spiritually.

"I WILL LOVE THEM"

Napoleon Bonaparte said, "Alexander, Caesar, Charlemagne, and I have all founded empires. But on what did we rest the creations of our genius? Upon force. Jesus Christ founded his empire on love; and at this hour millions of men would die for him."[8]

Leadership becomes extremely powerful and persuasive when the leader truly loves those He is leading. God not only wants you to *lead* your family but deeply love them. People tend to follow the teachings and leadership of those who love them the most.

The more you walk with God and obey Him each day, the more of His love will be "poured out" in your heart (Romans 5:5).

137

He will then increasingly deepen and enrich the love you already have for your family.

Love Them through Your Marriage

Children feel much more secure if they know their parents love each other. When they see you hold, kiss, and express affection for your wife, your children will stand taller in the day and sleep better in the night. But few things can break them down more than when Mom and Dad don't seem to care about each other.

If you are married, and your relationship with your wife is rocky or bland, you must do whatever it takes to put your marriage back on a sound footing. Swallow your pride. Work through your issues. Get godly counseling. Ask forgiveness for your part in any wrongdoing. Talk. Listen. Change.

Remember, *you are the man,* and God has placed you in the driver's seat to take the wheel on any issues harming your home or your marriage. Don't wait for her. Step up and be the leader God meant you to be. It's never easy, but that's why God gave this *courageous* assignment to you. (The next chapter should help you with this.)

If you are divorced, then acknowledge to your children that this was not the way you or God intended for your relationship to end. Ask for their forgiveness, and make the extra effort to show them in God's Word how to make a marriage work so the cycle of divorce does not continue to repeat itself.

Love Them through Words of Affirmation

Too many fathers find the words "I love you" difficult to say — even to their children — but it is absolutely necessary that they audibly hear the confirmation of their father's love. Even if you never or only rarely heard it from *your* father, look them in the eye and tell them how valuable they are to you. That you're grateful God gave them to you.

Your words in ten seconds can change them forever and build incredible strength in your son or daughter's sense of self-worth. A wise father will make sure his children have no doubt of their priceless value to him.

Love Them through Your Time

Words are important, but if your actions say otherwise, you're sending mixed signals that will crush their trust in you. This is especially critical in your work. You should do your job well, of course, performing it with excellence as unto the Lord. But your children need to know clearly that your work is not more important to you than they are. If your kids feel they always get your leftover energy and attention, they will disconnect and struggle with resentment.

But you can avoid this — as hard as it is — by putting limits on your time at work, delegating, and demonstrating that you will fight for your family. Certain seasons will crop up when work will demand more of your time than usual. But if this is always the pattern, continually an issue, then you're masking a problem of the heart behind your commitment to work, likely getting more of your needs met there than you're willing to admit. Your heart will follow your investment. Work will steal it away from your family if you let it.

Your children's level of confidence, security, and spiritual health are all connected to your influence in their lives, and your job doesn't have the right to steal that from them . . . or from you. They will not remember what you did *for* them while you were at work as much as what you did *with* them. And the example you set will likely be what they follow and display for their kids as well. Provide that loving example to them.

"I WILL PROTECT THEM"

Fathers are the primary protectors — physically, emotionally, and spiritually. For example, when a man walks his daughter down the aisle at her wedding, he should be communicating two key things to her and the others attending: first, that he has guarded her moral purity throughout her life for her husband (2 Corinthians 11:2), and second, that the man to which he is now giving his daughter has been proven morally, financially, and spiritually qualified to lead her, provide for her, and protect her from that day on.

Most men don't realize or recognize this awesome responsibility. But as a father, know that you are called to shepherd and protect your children in each area of their lives during the short time you have with them.

Jesus said, "When a strong man, fully armed, guards his own house, his possessions are undisturbed" (Luke 11:21). As the strong man of your home, you should lovingly keep your family from anything that will harm them in heart, mind, or body. A man should be aware, informed, and engaged in the lives of his wife and children — knowing what they're about, what they're thinking, who they're around, and what they're doing. He should prayerfully ask God to help him discern anything that might harm them or lead their hearts astray. Though this is time-consuming work, love drives men to guard what is valuable to them.

You should not only guard your own heart but your wife's as well. If the world is drawing her away from God's priorities for her life, or if something or someone is threatening her in any way, it is your job to step in and protect her. The same is true with your children. You'd like to think that your kids will make wise choices automatically without needing a lot of oversight and supervision. But they need help making the right decisions. That is why you are still their dad.

You may hope your wife will take care of these details so you can be free to do what you want to do. But being active on the front end as a father will pay off well and save you time and heartache on the back end.

This is why spending time in the Word with your family is so important. It teaches your children to love wisdom instead of developing a greater appetite for the world. Like sheep, your kids may want to wander into areas that are unsafe, and it is up to you to do what is necessary to ensure their well-being, even if they don't fully understand. If left alone, their tendency may be to lower their standards. But as their protective leader, your job is not just to give them boundaries but to use God's Word to teach them how to think wisely so they will set their own standards. Train them to fear and love God and not to "set foot on the path of the wicked or walk in the way of evil men" (Proverbs 4:14–15 NIV).

From the television, the Internet, and the movie screen — to their interactions with the opposite sex — you are responsible for framing the parameters and laying the ground rules. But of course, you need to be sure you're abiding by them too, not saying one thing while doing another. You must teach and train without hypocrisy. What you teach, you must live. You cannot tell your children to avoid drug and alcohol abuse if you are not. You cannot effectively warn them of the dangers of pornography if you are looking at it. You cannot urge them to save themselves for a godly marriage, treating their body as God's "temple" (1 Corinthians 6:19), when you are not loving your own wife as God commands with purity of thought and a carefully guarded heart. (Turn to page 383 in the appendix to see six of the most powerful influences you must guard in your children's lives.)

Yes, we all make mistakes and have fallen short of the glory of God, but your children can tell when your heart is sincere and purposefully living to please the Lord. Just ask yourself what you thought of your own parents. Very early on, you knew their level of integrity and honesty. You saw it, even when they didn't know you were looking. Your kids see it in you as well.

But by setting and modeling a high standard, you're protecting their hearts and working in their best interests. You're helping them not make avoidable and dangerous mistakes. You're guiding them in the way of lasting, lifelong truth. The older your kids get, the more they will need to understand the rationale behind your rules. Those that are rooted in the truths and principles of God will give them a strong foundation. As your kids learn to walk with God and know His character, they will discern why certain things are right and wrong, wise and unwise, better and best. This requires your courageous leadership!

"I WILL SERVE THEM"
When Jesus loved people, He identified their needs and then served them. He taught, healed, gave, worked, and led others in

service both to the Father and to mankind. He demonstrated the highest commands of Scripture: to love God with all your heart, soul, and strength, and to love your neighbor as yourself.

When you demonstrate the value of people by the way you serve others, your children will follow suit. If you do, they'll tend to embrace a lifestyle of generosity and self-sacrifice as being normal and second nature.

Teach your kids to think beyond themselves and find fulfillment in loving others through word and deed. Invite your kids to volunteer with you at church or at a charitable event. Help widows in your community or feed the homeless. This will grow their faith quicker than anything, as well as their understanding of how to love others, since experience is the most effective teacher.

You are the shepherd of your home. You are the main role model. When you love and serve, your children will learn to love and serve. When you guard your eyes, your mouth, and your mind, they are more likely to do the same. And when you pray for them regularly — for wisdom, for strength, for their hearts to be open to God and His Word — the Holy Spirit will take pleasure in helping you be the father and leader who shapes their lives today and impacts their world tomorrow.

Loving, protecting, serving, integrated with regular times of spiritual grounding — that's how men become the leaders in their homes, the champions of their wives, the heroes of their children, and the fruitful sons of their heavenly Father.

It takes strength. It takes courage. Lots of prayer and some unpopular stances. But you'll be able to look back on a family blessed by the initiative you invested and the priorities you kept in place. No man is perfect, but every man can be courageous.

Every man can lead his home with God's Word, God's presence, and God's help.

COURAGEOUS CHALLENGE

Begin the habit this week of reading
at least one chapter of God's Word
every day.

MEMORY VERSE

Have I not commanded you? Be strong
and courageous! Do not tremble or be
dismayed, for the LORD your God is with
you wherever you go. (Joshua 1:9)

Marriage is to be held in honor among
all, and the marriage bed is to be
undefiled; for fornicators and adulterers
God will judge.

Hebrews 13:4

CHAPTER 6
RESOLVE TO LOVE
YOUR WIFE

I WILL be faithful to my wife, to love and honor her, and be willing to lay down my life for her as Jesus Christ did for me.

A man of resolution needs to be faithful to his wife and to lead her with Christlike love. He should know that the greatest love, strongest marriages, and best sex are all found in the will of God and begin with the presence of God.

God alone designed the marvelous mystery of marriage. He owns the copyright and created it to be the most romantic, satisfying, and intimate relationship on earth. And when a man and his wife obey what God tells them to do, they will have significant breakthroughs in their marriage and more fully enjoy it and one another.

We're about to go deep now, so mentally hang on because you don't want to miss this. Even if you're unmarried, this could serve you well in the future.

Our journey to become godly husbands starts with the idea of *holiness.* When something is *holy,* think of it as being incredibly special and infinitely valuable. Holy things are *set apart* from common, ordinary use and kept separately in their special place of honor. Holy things are exceptional and incomparable.

God is holy. He has set Himself apart from His creation and from anything that is unholy. Part of His holiness is that there is nothing else like Him. He is infinitely higher than everything else. "For as the heavens are higher than the earth," He says, "so are My ways higher than your ways and My thoughts than your thoughts" (Isaiah 55:9).

But not only is *God* holy. Everything He *does* is holy. His Spirit is the *Holy* Spirit. His Word is like no other book, so it is called the *Holy* Scriptures or the *Holy* Bible. When we worship Him, we celebrate how immeasurably unique He is. King David said, "There is no one like you, O LORD, and there is no God but you" (1 Chronicles 17:20 NIV).

He is holy. He is set apart.

And that's not *all* He has "set apart."

In the Old Testament, the nation of Israel was special because they were God's holy people, *set apart* for His own purposes. Moses said, "For you are a people holy to the LORD your God. The LORD your God has chosen you out of all the peoples on the face of the earth to be his people, his treasured possession" (Deuteronomy 7:6 NIV).

Some people wonder why God gave Israel so many specific instructions and detailed commands in the Old Testament law. He wasn't trying to limit their freedom. He was actually setting them apart from all other nations by teaching them how to be better in every area of their lives. Healthy in what they ate and how they handled disease. Pure in how they dressed themselves and behaved sexually. Honorable in how they treated their wives and raised their children. He wanted their lives to be holy so that they would become more like Him — priceless, pure, and special.

Considering the holiness of God also reveals why Jesus' sacrifice on the cross was so significant. Think about it. Jesus alone is God's holy Son. He alone lived a sinless, holy life. And on the cross He shed His blood as a holy sacrifice — the only sacrifice acceptable enough to satisfy the righteous judgment of a holy God, so that we as unholy sinners could be completely forgiven and walk with Him. God "made Him who knew no sin to be sin on our behalf, so that we might become the righteousness of God in Him" (2 Corinthians 5:21).

See what holiness does? It makes things unique, like no other. It sets them apart. It keeps special things special.

Throughout the Scriptures, the great sin against anything that was considered holy was when it was mistreated and made worthless or common. After everything God had done to deliver His people and help them become holy, He hated when they forgot His mercy, rejected His standards, and shamefully lived like the world — when they squandered their priceless value and sinned against their bodies, their marriages, and their families. Their sin was wrong not merely because they damaged and demeaned themselves, but more importantly because they dishonored the surpassing worth of God. Any sin in us reveals that God is not as holy to us as He should be.

The word *profane* means to treat something holy as if it is unholy, removing it from its special position of honor, taking it outside its protective boundaries, mistreating it as common and ordinary. Imagine a soldier washing his car with the American flag, or a woman mud wrestling in her wedding dress. That's a form of *profanity*. When God says something is holy, He commands us to guard and protect it. If we mistreat it — if we profane it — we bring painful, devastating consequences on ourselves.

Holiness. It's not just a form of good behavior. It's a new way of looking at your wife.

And here's why.

HOLY MATRIMONY

When you got married, you were declaring your wife *holy* unto you. That doesn't mean she's perfect. But you set her apart in your eyes above all the other women on the face of the earth. She became your prized possession for you to cherish, love, and protect for the rest of your life. And it is your responsibility to guard and keep her in that holy place of honor. If you belittle her or treat her in harsh, unloving ways, you are not just acting badly. You are *profaning* the treasure God has given you.

Because your wife is holy. Uniquely yours.

This one reason is really why adultery is such an abominable sin. Being unfaithful to your wife profanes the beauty of marriage, the sacredness of sex, the covenant of love, and the holiness of God all at the same time. God in the Old Testament and Jesus

Christ in the New Testament have approved and endorsed only *one* sexual relationship — one man and one woman who are married to one another. He is not limiting a man's enjoyment of sex. He is protecting it. He is keeping it pure, holy, and special.

Because, yes, even *sex* is holy within your marriage.

Sex is God's priceless wedding gift for a man and his wife to enjoy after they have covenanted their lives together in marriage. And it is to be shared with no one else — not even in fantasy or imagination.

No movie, pornographic site, or adulterous affair could ever come close to the level of romance and pure passion God desires to be enjoyed within a healthy marriage. Described vividly in the Old Testament book of Song of Solomon, God's design for sex within marriage is pure, permissible, and honorable. It leaves a man and his wife satisfied, liberated, and unashamed. It begins with committed love, transitions into exhilarating joy, and then ends with sweet peace. No other sexual relationship outside of marriage comes with the same benefits or the same unpolluted and healthy results in the end.

Most men in our culture don't get this. They don't understand how special and unique God has designed sex to be. They allow themselves to develop sexual feelings for other people — sometimes multiple people — and in many cases choose to act on their lust. But to God, sex is very holy and is to be kept holy. And if we dishonor Him and our wives by not treating it as such, we will get what everyone else gets who mishandles God's gift — guilt, dysfunction, emptiness, and all kinds of shameful consequences. If, however, we view sex as a holy, priceless, exclusive treasure, we will honor God and more fully enjoy our wives.

That's because anything you do that profanes your wife not only hurts her but also hurts you, since the Scripture says she is "one flesh" with you (Matthew 19:6). Part of you. Failing to honor her harms your ability to live out your true purpose as a married man.

God created your marriage to be a living portrait on earth to reveal the loving relationship of Jesus Christ with His Bride, the church — those whom He has declared "holy" unto Him (Ephesians 1:4). Therefore, your role as the husband in marriage is to be like a giant neon sign that says, "Look at my relationship with my wife! This is what the sacrificial, unconditional love of Jesus Christ for His Bride looks like!"

So by treating your wife as holy, and sex as holy, and everything about your marriage as holy, you place yourself and your spouse on a path that leads to blessing, friendship, respect, satisfaction, fulfillment, and togetherness.

You experience what it really means to be in *holy matrimony.*

"TO LOVE AND HONOR HER"

With your wife's "holy" standing as a starting point, you can begin a change in your relationship that puts you not only in line with God's purposes for your marriage but also in an ideal position to bless your wife with your love and honor.

In the fifth chapter of Ephesians, the apostle Paul says:

> Husbands, love your wives, as Christ loved the church and gave himself up for her. . . . Husbands ought also to love their own wives as their own bodies. He who loves his own wife loves himself; for no one ever hated his own flesh, but nourishes and cherishes it, just as Christ also does the church. (vv. 25, 28–29)

God's calling for you as a husband was not to marry the woman you love, but to love the woman you married. And that can be a tall order sometimes. The task laid upon husbands to love their wives is actually more demanding than the task placed upon wives to "submit" to their husbands. Why? Because of who we're told to model our love after — Jesus Christ and His sacrificial death.

The example God gives husbands to follow is simply the most courageous and sacrificial act ever done in all human history.

Christ's love for the church is without limit. When Jesus died for His bride, she was dirty and sinful. She was acting like His enemy. Yet He still chose to love her and lay down His life for her — not in a quick, easy death but by allowing Himself to be mocked and beaten, then nailed to a Roman cross. Jesus, the one who deserved to suffer the least for human sin, paid the highest price to meet His bride's deepest need.

That's courageous love.

It's true that many husbands, in the face of a dramatic emergency, might choose to die for their wives. But Christ calls us to a deeper, more costly kind of death: "If anyone would come after me," He says, "let him deny himself and take up his cross *daily* and follow me" (Luke 9:24 NIV). It's not

157

about being willing to die for her in a blaze of glory, but rather to sacrifice our lives *every day* for her. As husbands, we are called to put to death our own selfish desires to meet our wife's deepest needs. To say "no" to what we want so we can say "yes" to what she needs.

That is Christlike love and leadership.

Our daily behavior around our wives cannot be based upon their actions or our feelings, because neither of those is always good. It should instead be founded on a higher standard. Jesus said, "This is My commandment, that you love one another, *just as I have loved you*" (John 15:12). Christ is the master of love and is commanding us to learn specifically from Him. To love like He loves. To revolutionize how we treat our wives by loving them the most when they deserve it the least. Does that exemplify your love for your wife?

- Do you typically only express kindness and affection to her when you feel like she's earned it? Or do you faithfully love her when she least deserves it?
- Does your love for her weaken when she lets you down? Or does it stay rock solid in the midst of marital storms?
- Do you love her relentlessly and un-

conditionally? Or is there something she could do that would cause you to give up on her and abandon your marriage? If you can name something — anything — then your love is not unconditional.

Society teaches us to love the lovable when we feel like it. They believe when people are obnoxious, ugly, irresponsible, or hurtful, it's all right to drop them off at the nearest exit. This kind of love says to follow the feelings of your heart. "I've fallen in love with you; let's get married." But then later, "I've fallen *out* of love with you; I want a divorce."

Marriage, however, is a God-ordained covenant that invites you to love an imperfect, sinful person with the love of Christ. Because that's how He loves you. His love finds every reason to start but finds no reason to stop. Paul said:

I am convinced that neither death, nor life, nor angels, nor principalities, nor things present, nor things to come, nor powers, nor height, nor depth, nor any other created thing, will be able to separate us from the love of God, which

is in Christ Jesus our Lord.
(Romans 8:38–39)

Your wife should feel that secure in your love.

If your marriage fails — or is failing — it likely comes down to one key reason: *you have not loved your wife like Christ loves the church.* Most marriage problems are usually the result of a wife's wounded reaction to poor leadership and lack of love from her husband. A man wants to love a woman who deeply respects and appreciates him, but the kind of man that a woman appreciates and respects is one who sacrificially loves her, who patiently honors her, who lays down his life for her. On a daily basis.

So how do we do that? The standard Jesus set for us seems far too hard to do, far too high to reach. That's because it is. The key to loving like Jesus is to understand that we cannot do it on our own. God Himself must become our never-ending Source of love. And He is more than able to do it — to be *through* us what we cannot be ourselves.

His love for us is based upon God's choice, commitment, and unchanging character, not on us. God loves us not because we are lovable but because He is so loving. Nothing we do can generate more love from

Him or take His love away from us — because it was never based upon *us* to begin with.

Jesus said, "As the Father has loved me, so have I loved you. Now remain in my love" (John 15:9 NIV). When we surrender ourselves to His lordship and let Him rule our lives, His Holy Spirit becomes our endless supply, pouring out the unconditional love of God into our hearts (Romans 5:5). Then the *fruit* of His Spirit — beginning with "love" (Galatians 5:22–23) — permeates our thoughts and attitudes, then dictates how we act and react to one another.

When a husband or wife follows the example of Jesus, amazing things begin to happen. We disconnect from our mate's imperfections and plug into God's unchanging nature. Instead of "I love you because . . ." we can honestly say, "I love you, period. I love you when you're beautiful to me and when you're not. I love you when you treat me well and when you don't. And I'm daily relying on God's unconditional love to pour through my life into you. For better or for worse, in sickness and in health, till death do us part — that's how much I love you."

What would happen in the next year if God's unconditional love became the foundation of your marriage? What if you began to pray, "Lord, love her through me!" It would make you more honoring. It would make you more loving. And it would make you more faithful.

"I WILL BE FAITHFUL"

Because marriage is so holy, and because of what it represents, and because you are commanded to love your wife unconditionally like Jesus, you should never sin against God and your marriage by committing adultery. It is *God's will* for us to "abstain from sexual immorality" (1 Thessalonians 4:3). If you reject this command, you are not "rejecting man but the God who gives His Holy Spirit to you" (1 Thessalonians 4:8).

When a man commits adultery, every area of his life — body, soul, and spirit — experiences the harmful consequences. God has placed the exciting fire of sexual intimacy within the protective fireplace of the marriage bed, not only because He wants us to keep it holy, but also to keep us from getting burned. When taken outside of our marriage, the fire of sex will consume us and destroy the most precious things in our lives.

That's why God can say, "Whoever commits adultery with a woman lacks understanding; He who does so destroys his own soul. Wounds and dishonor he will get, and his reproach will not be wiped away" (Proverbs 6:32–33 NKJV).

Let's face it. Most men who fall into adultery do not originally set out to do so. They don't lose their marriages in a day. It starts off innocently, with small compromises that eventually became tolerated over time. A man gets too busy and isn't spending time with God in His Word. He gets worn out at work, then into a disagreement with his wife, and they go to bed angry. She begins to withdraw emotionally and physically, treating him with increasing disrespect. Then the Devil provides him opportunities to lust after other women — whether over the Internet or perhaps one woman in particular with whom he shares the frustrations he's having in his marriage. Soon he begins to pursue sexual fulfillment that is not from his wife. And before he knows it, he has baby-stepped his way into an addiction or an adulterous pit, unintentionally devastating his marriage, his spiritual walk, and the respect of his kids. He looks up one day to see a fool in the mirror and wonders how he got there.

But it's no real surprise. Lack of love, lack

of honor, lack of understanding for the holiness of marriage — they inevitably lead us to places we would never go in our right mind.

So because the issue of faithfulness can become one of the key struggles in a man's heart, and because it is so foundational to the sacred honor of marriage, and because our Enemy is so adept and deceptive at luring men away from their vows and commitments, lock down these ten action points for staying faithful in your heart and in your marriage — for keeping your wife "holy" in your sight. They're critical to your success:

1. *Stay in close fellowship with God.* Nothing is more powerful than an intimate, obedient relationship with God to satisfy the longings of your heart and help you overcome any temptation. Plugging into the vine of Christ empowers you to bear much fruit and avoid sin. A man who stays in God's Word daily and cries out to Him in prayer will have stronger discernment, greater love for his wife, and the grace to resist temptation. Stay close!

2. *Stay in close fellowship with your wife.* Maintain a fierce loyalty to her by putting new habits into place that draw you together. Call her from work. Turn off the TV and talk with her at night. Work through

problems instead of avoiding them. Apologize often and forgive without hesitation. Take her out on a date as often as you can. Go through the *Love Dare* book. Speak highly of her in public. Attend a marriage enrichment weekend together. Always be a student of books or seminars that can help you have a stronger marriage. Pray together. Laugh together. Love together. Bloom her with your love!

3. *Avoid lust and pornography like the plague.* Jesus said if a man looks at a woman with lust for her, he has already committed adultery in his heart (Matthew 5:27–28). Instead we must be like Job, who made a "covenant" with his eyes that he would not look lustfully at other women (Job 31:1), because lust is never satisfied and leads only to more lust and dissatisfaction. One of its biggest traps, of course, is pornography, which is all too available on the Internet and is currently perverting minds, darkening hearts, and weakening marriages by the millions. Viewing pornography is like eating out of a sewer. The only person you should see undressed before your eyes or in your imagination is your wife. Period. (If you or your friends are addicted to pornography, then see page 415 for some trusted tips on putting an end to its hold on your heart.)

4. *Never let your guard down.* Solomon (the wisest man in the Bible), Samson (the strongest man in the Bible), and David (the man after God's own heart) all fell the same way: women and sex. And if it could happen to them when they let their guards down, it can happen to you too. Whether you've been married for two weeks or forty years, you should always be on guard, maintaining a healthy fear of God and disgust with evil. Don't trust your flesh to do the right thing because it is sure to betray you. Be aware that when you are fearful, frustrated, or fatigued, you are most vulnerable. Avoid tempting situations rather than trying to resist temptation. Set wise standards as to what media you will view. Avoid being alone in a room or in a car with another woman. Purity comes only to those who truly want it and tenaciously guard it.

5. *Lead your heart.* Your heart will naturally chase after whoever looks good or appeals to you at the moment. So even though you should always treat women with respect, you must keep any woman other than your wife at a healthy emotional distance. Foolish men today are reconnecting with old girlfriends on social networking sites, not guarding their hearts, and then bailing on their marriages. Stay away from anyone who

causes sparks because you *will* get burned. Our hearts can be selfish, deceptive, and very sinful. Don't follow your heart; lead it. The more you pray for your wife, focus on her positive attributes, and invest in your marriage, the more your heart will turn toward her.

6. *Seriously consider the consequences.* Solomon, son of King David and Bathsheba, grew up knowing and seeing how his parents' one-night stand eventually led to the murder of Bathsheba's husband, the death of their illegitimate child, the immoral life of David's son Absalom, the loss of twenty thousand men in battle, and shame to the people of God. The immediate thrill of illicit sexual excitement is always followed by devastating, long-lasting consequences. Then the adulterer will conclude that those short minutes of pleasure were not worth the years of pain afterward. That's when the "Affair to Remember" becomes the "Fornication I Can't Forget." (Turn to page 387 for a lengthy list of consequences that result from adultery. Read them with fear and trembling. Remember them when adultery comes knocking.)

7. *Run for the hills.* The Bible commands us to "flee immorality" (1 Corinthians 6:18). Only a fool says, "I can handle

temptation without sinning." The wise man says, "I'm not going anywhere near it." Whether it be a female coworker with flirty eyes, the TV in a hotel room, or an unfiltered Internet site, if it even *barely* starts to trip you up, get away from it as fast as you can. Establish some hard and fast rules, like, "No television or computer viewing after your wife's in bed." If you are falling, get rid of whatever's tripping you up. Guard what's holy and priceless!

8. *Lock shields with other men.* Proverbs 18:1 says that when a man gets alone and away from others, he tends to do two unhealthy things: he "seeks his own desire," and he "quarrels against all sound wisdom." Since we are in a moral battle, we need other soldiers around us, men who can help us become better and stronger. By working together and being honest, men can help each other with their struggles, encourage their daily walk, warn against doing stupid things, and then provide counsel toward becoming more successful in marriage. Find some good men around you and start meeting for workouts, breakfast, Bible study, or prayer together. "As iron sharpens iron, so one man sharpens another" (Proverbs 27:17 NIV).

9. *Don't let divorce become an option.*

Adultery can obviously lead to a divorce, but Jesus pointed out how divorce can lead to adultery. "It was said, 'Whoever sends his wife away, let him give her a certificate of divorce'; but I say to you that everyone who divorces his wife, except for the reason of unchastity, makes her commit adultery; and whoever marries a divorced woman commits adultery" (Matthew 5:31–32). Many couples get a divorce because they're not happy. But selfishness is never satisfied. Marriage is about *love,* not happiness — love that is unselfish and "does not seek its own" (1 Corinthians 13:5). If your relationship is not what it should be, how willing are you to get help to avoid divorce? What if it costs time and money for counseling or a marriage conference? Be willing to sacrifice and invest in it. God can resurrect any marriage if a couple will just die to themselves.

10. *Have better sex with your wife more often.* God's solution to sexual immorality is marriage (1 Corinthians 7:1–5). Meeting one another's sexual needs helps us avoid Satan's temptations toward immorality. But remember that your level of enjoyment during sex is more about what's going on in your heart, mind, and spirit than in your body. Too often we don't prepare ourselves emotionally, spiritually, and relationally for

sex, then we wonder why the act itself is only marginally satisfying. Since the sexual relationship is founded upon your commitment, love, and intimacy, it is important to get all three of these things right before you are physically together. (See page 391 for seven steps to better sex with your wife.)

In conclusion, God can give you an incredibly satisfying marriage. He is in the business of resurrecting dead marriages and strengthening good ones. Many marriages once destroyed by affairs, pornography, bitterness, alcoholism, or drug abuse have been restored after a man and his wife have been willing to get honest before God about their past failures, repent of their sins, forgive one another, and then recommit themselves to the ways of God.

But let it start with you. Resolve to be a faithful husband, an honoring husband, a loving husband, one who lays down his life for the one he declared "holy" to himself at the wedding altar. Be the Christlike leader of your marriage. Give this relationship to the Lord, resolve to be faithful with it, and watch Him transform it into a wonderful adventure of lifelong love!

COURAGEOUS CHALLENGE

Set up one or more new protective moral boundaries in your life this week to help you guard your heart and your marriage.

MEMORY VERSE

Marriage is to be held in honor among all, and the marriage bed is to be undefiled; for fornicators and adulterers God will judge. (Hebrews 13:4)

May God Almighty bless you and make you fruitful and multiply you, that you may become a company of peoples. May He also give you the blessing of Abraham, to you and to your descendents with you.

Genesis 28:3–4

Chapter 7
Resolve to Bless Your Children

I WILL bless my children and teach them to love God with all of their hearts, all of their minds, and all of their strength.

Every little boy in a baseball uniform who steps up to the plate to face a pitcher will lift his bat with hope. But the intensity of that hope depends on the level of his self-confidence.

Many go to bat just hoping they don't strike out or get hit in the head. Some hope the pitcher will walk them to first. Others are only hoping they somehow hit the ball — somewhere, anywhere.

But imagine a boy whose father currently plays in the major leagues. He's watched his dad round the bases in massive stadiums before thousands of cheering fans. He knows the players on his father's team by name. He was swinging plastic bats in the backyard when he was in diapers. Baseball is in his blood.

As he steps up to the plate and looks over to see his dad cheering him on from the stands, he lifts his bat with a greater vision of success in his eyes. He knows he's knocking this next pitch over the center fielder's head.

He truly believes he can do it.

And this swing, this game, is only the beginning. He sees himself playing baseball in high school, college, and even the big leagues. His dad has told him he can. He's heard his father's vivid stories of sacrifice, hard work, and adventure on the way to playing professionally. His dad has put up posters of the all-time greats on his son's bedroom wall and spent hours with him in the batting cage. He's committed to walking his namesake through every step of the journey, to do whatever he can to make success happen for his son.

This is what it looks like to have a higher definition of success than most people in the world. And this is what it looks like to have the blessing of your father.

Too many parents have very low standards when it comes to defining success for their children. Some just want them not to mess up their lives. Others hope they will graduate from college and find a decent job.

Although this sounds noble, it is not impressive in God's eyes. That's like hoping your son just gets to first base.

But what should success look like for your children? Do they know? Have you told them and talked about it? Have they seen you modeling it yourself?

This fourth point of *Resolution* is about getting God's vision inside their heads . . . by resolving to get inside their hearts.

REAL-LIFE SUCCESS

When Moses stood before the nation of Israel to give his final speech before he died, he boldly redefined success for them. "You shall love the LORD your God with all your heart and with all your soul and with all your might" (Deuteronomy 6:5).

Jesus later referred to this as the greatest commandment of all time. Through this, God is calling us to do the greatest thing (to love) toward the greatest One (God Himself) in the greatest way (with all that we are). If anyone finds worldly fame and prosperity but misses out on this, he actually misses everything. It is God's will that we love Him, obey Him, and live for Him. He should always be our greatest priority and our first love.

But not only is this how we define success

175

for ourselves; this is how we are called as fathers to define success for our children and grandchildren. To see them living for Christ and making Him known through their lives is infinitely more important than their success on the ball field or in the classroom, more important than any award they may receive, more important than landing an impressive job or making a lot of money.

To love God and do His will is to succeed in life. Period.

But this message is more than just information for our kids to download or a sentence for us to say one or two times and hope they get it. Moses told us precisely how to instill this truth into our children's lives:

> These words, which I am commanding you today, shall be on your heart. You shall teach them diligently to your sons and shall talk of them when you sit in your house and when you walk by the way and when you lie down and when you rise up. (Deuteronomy 6:6–7)

Two takeaways from this. *First, God's Word must "be on your heart."* Children who forsake the faith are usually those who did not see God actively working in their parents' lives. But they develop an appetite for God when they see their dad and mom truly loving Him and walking with Him, when they see the blessings and rewards of your obedience firsthand. Whether it's delighting in His creation, enthusiastically telling them stories from His Word, or celebrating His goodness in ordinary conversation, you should delight in the Lord around your kids. You can't inspire them with truths you're not living yourself.

So when God answers your prayers, tell your kids about it. When He changes your heart or helps you overcome temptation, celebrate it with them. When you face a season of suffering or persecution, let them see the strength of your faith. Point out how He works. In your own life. In your own words.

One clearly answered prayer can powerfully instill faith toward God in the heart of your child. One humbly confessed mistake can help them see the everyday reality of God's redemption. Every day gives you fresh, new material for making your life with Christ a front-row experience for the whole family. Let them see that loving Him is what gets you out of bed in the morning.

Second, training your children to love God

177

must occur within the context of close relationships. It must be part of your daily interactions with them — when greeting your kids at the breakfast table, sitting around the house, having spiritually rich conversations in the car or at dinner, praying together before going to sleep each night.

Help them fall in love with God!

You don't have to be eloquent or seminary trained to do this. It's those "Did you know . . ." or "Hey, by the way . . ." moments that mean the most to your kids — things you talk about while you're out in the yard, heading to the store, or working on a project together.

Making disciples of all nations begins with your own children. By talking with your kids about Him through the day, and then (most important) modeling a love for Him in your own life, you set up your sons and daughters for long-term, multigenerational success.

But it all starts with their hearts.

HEART TO HEART

One of the most important ingredients for successful parenting is having your children's hearts. Research shows that Christians are theologically losing the next generation. More than 90 percent of born-again kids today are rejecting the absolute truth their parents embrace. Respected apologist Josh McDowell explains it this way: "You can be the greatest explainer of truth. But if the very heart of your son or daughter does not believe 'my daddy loves me,' they will walk away from your truth."[9]

People tend to embrace the teaching and beliefs of those who love them the most. And your children are no different. They are much more likely to accept the truth you teach if you deliver it to them within a loving, heart-to-heart relationship. Whoever has their heart has their ears.

This sheds light on why God ended the Old Testament with the need to "restore the hearts of the fathers to their children and the hearts of the children to their fathers" (Malachi 4:6). When this doesn't happen, fathers invite the "curse" of broken relationships into their homes and truth is forsaken. So the success of Christian families truly depends on parents learning to shepherd the hearts of their children.

One of the greatest challenges to any father is knowing how to properly wield his authority — how to be a gracious servant-leader rather than a demanding tyrant. Some fathers are content with outward obedience only. The heart doesn't really matter. They just want their kids to behave.

But children in that situation will jump at the chance to disobey when their dad isn't around. They'll go elsewhere to find their affirmation — from the wrong people in the wrong places.

You can tell when a father doesn't have his kids' hearts. You sense the disrespect and anger, the bitterness and emotional distance. The kids don't want to be around him. They no longer listen to him. But children who trust their dad's counsel and leadership are those whose fathers have been proactive in winning their hearts. "Give me your heart, my son," Solomon said to his own child, "and let your eyes delight in my ways" (Proverbs 23:26).

Dr. S. M. Davis wisely explains it like this:

The key ingredient in raising good children is to get their hearts early, keep their hearts, and be extremely vigilant not to lose your children's hearts. If you do lose your child's heart, then quickly find out where and when you lost it, and put into action a plan to get their heart back no matter what it takes to do it. No matter how much time or trouble or money it takes to get back your child's heart, you must decide ahead of time that you will be willing to pay the price.[10]

You know how to do this if you've ever dated or courted someone. You can tell if her heart is with you or not. You know when something is not right, when the connection between you is strained. If this is a relationship you really want to pursue, you'll talk as long as she needs, go the extra mile, fulfill any promise, do whatever it takes to make sure you have her heart and she knows she has yours.

Why should your relationship with your children be any different?

Jesus was so loyal to His heavenly Father that He was able to say, "Whatever the Father does, these things the Son also does in like manner" (John 5:19). And here's why: "For the Father loves the Son, and shows Him all things that He Himself is doing" (John 5:20). The Father knew the heart of His Son, and the Son entrusted His heart to the Father.

How well do you have your children's hearts?

How sure are your children that they have yours?

How Fathers Lose Hearts

Despite this, fathers are notorious for doing things that anger their children and lose their hearts. Ephesians 6:4 says, "Fathers, do not provoke your children to anger, but bring them up in the discipline and instruction of the Lord." Colossians 3:21 says, "Fathers, do not exasperate your children, so that they will not lose heart." Before telling us to train and instruct our children, we are warned not to frustrate or embitter them. Why?

Because if we lose their hearts, we lose everything. They simply won't listen to us. This is so important that if it is not heeded, fathering will fail.

Intimacy is tied to feeling emotionally safe around someone. If your kids get angry with you and you don't resolve it, their hearts will close off to you and become bitter. Then the Devil will begin to fill their minds with accusations against you. He will develop a "list of crimes" in their thoughts of wrongs you have committed, then he will use this list to help them justify rebellion against you.

So when your children get angry with you, you need to stop what you are doing, get engaged, and help them deal with their anger until it is gone. You cannot live in denial and tolerate even one barrier that chokes out your ability to influence them for good.

Here is a list of ten things that fathers do to anger and lose the hearts of their children. Seriously consider these to see if any of them are present in your relationship with your child. Work hard to eliminate the following "heart hindrances" that will push them away.

1. *Your absence.* Whether a man abandons his kids all at once or is never home because he's always working, he still leaves them as sheep without a shepherd. This sends the signal to your kids, "You're not important enough for me to prioritize you, spend time with you, or really care about what's going on in your life."

2. *Your anger.* Proverbs 27:4 says that wrath is cruel. When you react in anger, you can thoughtlessly say or do things in the heat of the moment that deeply wound your son or daughter's spirit long-term, which can cause them to withdraw from you. Love is slow to anger. But if you blow your top, then humble yourself and quickly apologize. Too much is at stake!

3. *Unjust discipline.* Children can sour if they feel discipline is unjustified or administered unfairly. Parents must explain rules

and consequences clearly using God's Word and authority rather than their opinion (Ephesians 6:1–3). Every time you discipline, ask yourself, "How can I train them without losing their heart?"

4. *Harsh criticism.* Dads can sometimes be unnecessarily hard on their kids. What seems like a small chisel of criticism to you can feel like a crushing hammer to them. Never call your children names or embarrass them in public. Don't be sarcastic or belittling. Show them how to laugh at themselves and learn. Kids who have no freedom to fail will tend to rebel when given any freedom at all.

5. *Lack of compassion.* Mercy warms hearts; carelessness distances them. Children can get worked up about temporary, pressing matters — school, friends, feelings, competitions. We must provide a listening ear, wise counsel, prayerful support, and a willing hand. Rescuing your kids during times of panic makes you their hero! Help them think of you as an oasis they can run to, not a dry desert that offers no relief.

6. *Favoritism.* Less favored children become resentful. Favoritism and jealousy in Scripture led Rachel and Leah to fight and Joseph's brothers to hate him. You may not feel like you play favorites — but perception

is reality to your children if they think you do. Every one of your children should know that you have no favorites, but if you did, it would probably be them because of your great love for them.

7. *Hypocrisy.* No one is perfect, but preaching one thing while doing another, breaking promises, and refusing to apologize will kill trust between you and your children. When they identify hypocrisy in you, be quick to repent, turning from your sin and seeking God's forgiveness along with your family's.

8. *Hurting their mother.* Whether through divorce, adultery, or mistreatment, children feel confused and betrayed when their father hurts their mother. They will tend to take up offense for the woman who loves them. Since they are commanded by God to honor their mother, you need to defend her, not attack her. If you teach them to dishonor her, they will eventually dishonor you.

9. *Misunderstanding.* Rebellion is often tied to kids feeling misunderstood and not listened to by their parents. When children open up, parents need to listen carefully and then communicate back to the child what they have heard before sharing their own opinions or disagreeing with them. If a matter is important to them, it should be important to you. Tune in.

10. *Unrealistic expectations.* Children will become quickly discouraged if they believe their parents have set them up to fail. Avoid comparing their weaknesses with another child's strengths or expecting them to act as maturely as you. Parents are to find how God has "wired" their child and develop that "wiring" rather than forcing them to become something God never intended for them to become. If your child believes he can't please you, he'll eventually quit trying.

Let these ten warnings signs help you avoid future pitfalls and also motivate changes that will draw your children back into your arms. As a father, you must keep your radar up to sense if you have your children's hearts. Periodically ask them things like . . .

- Have I ever wounded you and not made it right?
- Have I said one thing and done another?
- Have I made promises and not kept them?
- Is there anything you're angry with me about?
- Is there anything you're not telling me because you're afraid?

Your kids may be able to present you with a "list of crimes" that have wronged or angered them. Find out. Be ready to write them down, work through them, and apologize so you can let the healing begin.

A friend of ours was sitting with his family at a father-daughter banquet held by their church. Someone at the table asked one of the girls what her father had done that made the biggest impression on her. She said, "I remember one time when Dad was harsh with me. Then a few minutes later he came back into my room, and he cried and asked my forgiveness. I've never forgotten that."

God can graciously redeem our many failures for good, provided we recognize those failures and confess them. Too many men foolishly refuse to apologize because they're trying to save face and don't want to look bad. But their pride is only making matters worse. Dads who admit their shortcomings don't lose their children's trust. They gain it.

And as we work through and turn off the bad stuff, we should also turn on the good stuff.

Capturing Your Children's Hearts

Regardless of the age of your kids, you need to throw on the brakes and start spending more "heart to heart" time with them. Even if they're not receptive initially. Even if trust needs to be rebuilt. Even if your children are grown and gone, your pursuit of their hearts must still go on.

It's time to turn the corner. To remember that teaching your children to love God cannot happen when you're not loving them well yourself. It's time to clear out all the noise and discontent that's created so much uncomfortable space between you and your children. Here are three powerful rivers that need to be unleashed and allowed to flow freely from your heart to theirs.

Attention

Too many moments at home have found us busy while our children have waited in the shadows. They won't wait forever. Too often we've allowed good things to steal us away from the *best* things — those priceless, unrecoverable moments with our kids while they're growing up. We have a culture of men who ignore and don't talk to their children. And this needs to change starting now.

We should daily engage them, laugh with

them, comfort them, and walk with them throughout life. "Tell me how you are doing." "What have you been up to lately?" "What are you most excited about right now?" These are questions dads should ask often. We should make it clear to them that they can always come to us and talk about anything.

Some fathers take each of their children out for breakfast for a little one-on-one time with Dad. Daughters love date nights, and sons relish a "Men's Night Out." Whether it's riding bikes together, reading books, playing sports, or sitting at a coffee shop, time out with Dad can open up conversations you wouldn't usually have at home with your kids.

Brooks Adams, son of Charles Adams, U.S. Ambassador to Great Britain under the Lincoln Administration, was only eight years old when he wrote in his diary one afternoon, "Went fishing with my father; the most glorious day of my life." Unaware of this, his dad also kept a diary, and he too had marked a comment about that same day and event. "Went fishing with my son; a day wasted."[11]

He missed the significance of that day.

How many more days might they have spent together if this father knew how much it meant to his little boy? How many times have we considered it a "waste" to push our kids on the swing at the playground or to bring them a snack and a kiss on the head while they're busy doing homework? Yet we find time to watch television, or surf the Web, or whatever else we deem valuable and necessary to us. We need to look back at Scripture, understand the job God has given us, and redefine the difference between "wasted" time and priceless investments.

Affirmation

Both children and adults want the approval and praise from their dads. They want their father's "blessing" in their lives. To *bless* means "to speak well of." When you bless your children, you are lovingly using your God-given authority to verbally affirm them toward future success.

God told Moses that the high priest should bless the sons of Israel by saying, "The LORD bless you, and keep you; the LORD make His face shine on you, and be gracious to you; the LORD lift up His countenance on you, and give you peace" (Numbers 6:24–26). Then God said, "So they shall invoke My name on the sons of Israel, and I then will bless them" (Numbers 6:27).

When Jesus was baptized, a voice from heaven said, "You are My beloved Son, in You I am well-pleased" (Mark 1:11). God the Father was publicly affirming His Son by speaking love and acceptance over Him. He also invested in Jesus at that moment by sending His Holy Spirit down to Him. This not only encouraged Jesus but set Him up for complete success to do the will of His heavenly Father throughout His earthly ministry.

As you learn to bless your children, this will become a powerful experience for them. It is important that you communicate to them, "You are my son (daughter) and I dearly love you. I am very pleased with you." You should then follow up by investing in their future. You should pray for them, encourage them, introduce them to the right people, and give them what they need to help them be successful. Even adult men and women long for their father's blessing if they never received it growing up.

If you didn't receive your father's blessing, then you must discover that men who are surrendered to Jesus Christ share in the blessing Jesus received from His Father. Scripture says we are blessed "in Him" with every spiritual blessing and are "accepted and beloved" (Ephesians 1:1–14). Receive this blessing from your heavenly Father by faith, and then model it to your children. Anytime you greet them or talk to them, your countenance, the look in your eyes, and your tone of voice either says, "You are a delight to me" or "You are an irritation to me." You should praise them privately, one-on-one, and publicly in front of others. "That is awesome! You are really good at that," needs to come from your lips as their biggest cheerleader. Regardless of your past, step up to do this now!

Affection

Our heavenly Father pours out His uncon-ditional love on us (Romans 5:5), and so should we to our sons and daughters. What a tragedy to hear grown men confess that their fathers were never loving or affection-ate. Jesus reached out and touched with love. So should we. Whether you received love from your father or not, you need to pour it out affectionately on your kids. *Break this chain.* Make sure they know deeply in their hearts that you care for them. Hug them, kiss them, hold them close. Interact with them in ways that make them fully see, hear, and feel your love.

A child needs not only the discipline of a

father but also his warm affection and tender love. When they are little, tickle them, kiss them, wrestle with them, and carry them proudly on your shoulders. As they grow up, don't stop embracing them and putting your arm around them.

Boys who feel loved by their dads are bolder, stronger, kinder to others, and more secure in their manhood. Girls who feel valued by their dads are more radiant, less desperate for a boyfriend, and more careful whom they marry. So invest in them, take them places, flood them with tender affection, leaving no question in their minds about your genuine love for them. One of the most painful regrets any man has as he ends his life is the love he withheld from others that were close to him. Love now so you can die without this regret.

God has given us a powerful and amazing calling to bless our children and grandchildren and to teach them to love Him with all their hearts and lives. But they will not be drawn to believe what we say if we don't speak it from within the context of a loving relationship with them. Our love touches them deeply and opens their hearts to hear truth and follow their heavenly Father faithfully. Then they will likely pass on our blessing to *their* kids.

So let's step up to the plate with a new vision for success. And let's boldly knock it out of the park for the sake of Christ and many generations to come!

COURAGEOUS CHALLENGE

Talk with your kids this week and "bless" them by telling them how much you love them and are proud of them.

MEMORY VERSE

Give me your heart, my son, and let your eyes delight in my ways. (Proverbs 23:26)

Remember also your Creator in the days of your youth. . . . Fear God and keep his commandments, for this is the whole duty of man.

Ecclesiastes 12:1, 13 (ESV)

CHAPTER 8
RESOLVE TO LIVE
WITH HONOR

I WILL train them to honor authority and
live responsibly.

Jesus said to make disciples of all peoples
and all nations. This is our awesome, lifelong, privileged calling. So world evangelism
and biblical training should be taking place
among the nations, across the street, and in
the privacy of our own families at home.
However, as previously stated, somewhere
between eighty and ninety percent of kids
in America are abandoning their parents'
faith once they reach adulthood. At that
tragic rate, the fifty million children who
are growing up in church today would die
out to fewer than *seven thousand* in only
ten generations' time. That's sadly where
current Christian families in America are
headed without a radical change of leadership and direction.

But if parents learned to win their children's hearts and train them and their grandkids faithfully, like Deuteronomy 6 commands, great things could happen through generational discipleship. Think about this concept. If you and your wife had two children and trained them to faithfully live for Christ, and both of them raised two more children to faithfully live for Christ as well, then those same ten generations could produce 1,024 faithful believers — just from your family alone. If there were four children (instead of two) in each family, the total rises above 260,000. If there were six children in each generation, it could mean more than ten million followers of Christ — again, from your one family alone.

This is more than a math lesson. This is a powerful reminder that your influence — for good or bad — lasts much longer than the few years your children are under your roof. Realize that when you speak into your children's ears, you are speaking into the ears of your great-great-grandchildren as well.

So when the Scriptures tell you to teach the Word "diligently" to your children "when you sit in your house and when you walk by the way and when you lie down and when you rise up" (Deuteronomy 6:7), the ramifications are both extreme and extensive. Raising kids who love the Lord is a true game-changer. And if your children are grown and gone, then start praying for them now and pouring into your grandkids as well.

What and how should we be training our kids? According to the Bible, there's another important element — besides love — that we must intentionally teach and model to our children and grandchildren: the instruction "to *fear* the LORD your God, to keep all His statutes and His commandments" (Deuteronomy 6:2). If they are going to study, know, obey, and follow God's Word with their lives, then we must teach them to *fear the Lord.*

Love, truth, and respectful fear go hand in hand.

THE FEAR OF THE LORD

God is love, but He is also to be feared. The fear of the Lord is a holy, reverent respect for God that causes us to take Him very, very seriously, realizing He is all-knowing, all-powerful, and completely holds our lives, our universe, our judgment, and our eternal destiny in His hands.

To fear Him is to be soberly aware of His awesome authority over us, not going around thinking we can do whatever we want without real side-effects or consequences. As a result, fearing the Lord keeps a child's and a man's desires and life in check.

Fearing the Lord transforms our thinking. It is a blessing and a protection to us.

It causes us to guard what we say and helps us make wise decisions about what we do. It motivates a person not to steal, sleep around, or abuse his body with drugs and alcohol — because he knows a holy God is watching over him at all times and will judge him one day for his actions.

King Solomon explained that "by the fear of the Lord one keeps away from evil" (Proverbs 16:6). It is a "fountain of life" through which "one may avoid the snares of death" (14:27).

So don't think of it as an anchor to carry around or a dark cloud of dread that takes all the fun out of life. The fear of the Lord actually causes our other fears to go away. It brings "strong confidence" (14:26). It doesn't just keep us from negative burdens; it opens the floodgates for positive blessings.

- Wisdom, counsel, and understanding begin with the fear of the Lord. (Proverbs 8:14)

- Wealth, honor, and fruitfulness follow the fear the Lord. (Proverbs 8:17–19)
- Its fruits include humility and a proper hatred of pride and evil. (Proverbs 8:13)
- God's presence, provision, and blessing are granted to those who fear Him. (Psalm 34:9)

Maintaining a fear of the Lord actually helps us enjoy better and longer lives!

> Come, you children, listen to me;
> I will teach you the fear of the LORD.
> Who is the man who desires life and loves length of days that he may see good? Keep your tongue from evil and your lips from speaking deceit. Depart from evil and do good; seek peace and pursue it. (Psalm 34:11–14)

The fear of the Lord impacts future generations. It keeps us and our families engaged in things that lead to blessing. "How blessed is the man who fears the LORD, who greatly delights in His commandments. His descendants will be mighty on earth; the generation of the upright will be blessed" (Psalm 112:1–2).

It is for this reason that we should prayerfully ask God to help us develop a strong fear of the Lord in our lives and in our children. Training them to fear the Lord sets them up to live with incredible wisdom and success.

So teach them to take God seriously, to know He is omniscient and always watching them (Proverbs 15:3). To know they will reap what they sow (Galatians 6:7). To know He will judge them one day (Romans 14:12). And to know He is a great rewarder of those who diligently seek Him and obey Him (Hebrews 11:6).

To fear Him — just like to love Him — is a very, very good thing!

And as this sense of godly respect grows on us and our children, as we balance our love for Him with our healthy fear of Him, it naturally leads to something that is sorely missing in our society today — something each of us as men desire deeply to recapture and restore.

That "something" is *honor.*

HONOR

In years past, men would shake hands on an agreement and would keep their word. Being honorable was important to them. They took it seriously. Not that people in past generations had everything together, but when Christian influence was the norm, they were generally more attuned to what it meant to have a reputation as an honest, respectable man.

They valued honor.

When you see a row of soldiers standing at attention, with uniforms in pristine condition and an expression of resolution on their faces, it stirs something within you. Their very behavior raises the level of honor you feel for your country and your flag. These men are ready to defend, fight for, and represent their nation. They are disciplined and trained. They understand the necessity of carrying out orders and fulfilling their duty. There's a confidence in their walk and a strength in their manner. They exude *honor,* and it makes those around them want to get their act together and raise their own level of respect.

Honor makes a man stand up straighter.

Walk taller. Win favor. Excel faster.

To live with honor means you adopt a higher standard. You rise above the status quo and reflect a system of values bigger than you are as an individual. You keep your word and esteem other people highly. You avoid the shortcuts that would damage your integrity, and you focus on your duties with disciplined intention. You show respect. No matter how other people around you are behaving, you maintain your stance of honor.

And fathers should learn to pass down these same qualities to their kids so they too can model what it means to live holy and honorably before the Lord.

When children understand they've been created by a powerful, intentional God who knows them personally and desires to use them for His glory, this knowledge adds honor and purpose to every cell in their bodies. And when you train your children to treat God and all people with great respect and honor, you set them up to be greatly respected and honored and more influential.

An honorable young man keeps his word and fulfills his responsibilities. He learns to give up his chair to the elderly, avert his eyes away from immorality, and communicate with clarity. An honorable young lady learns to listen attentively, dress modestly, and speak respectfully and graciously. We instill this in our children partly through character training and partly through teaching them basic etiquette.

Honor is attractive. It doesn't demand respect; it quickly earns it.

Fear grounds us.

Honor inspires us.

And one of the first places we teach these things and see them in action is in our and our children's relationship with authority.

"I WILL TRAIN THEM TO HONOR AUTHORITY"

No one likes to see blue lights in his rear-view mirror, but if you're speeding or breaking traffic laws, you're accountable to them because they represent authority over you.

If your boss calls you into his office at work to reprimand you for an action you've taken, you may or may not feel like his rebuke is warranted. But he is in authority over you, and you are accountable to honor him.

The whole concept of authority comes from God. Earthly authority is His design and tool for creating order and for keeping us accountable and responsible, for honoring good and for punishing evil (Romans 13:1–4). Authorities on earth help keep us mindful of His superior, eternal authority — and to prepare us for the day when we stand before Him in judgment.

Since God can turn the heart of anyone in a leadership position in any direction (Proverbs 21:1) and replace a leader at any moment, we should be like Jesus and submit to our imperfect, human authorities knowing that God uses them to carry out His purposes (John 19:11). The only time we should *not* submit to them is when they are asking us to disobey God and sin (Acts 5:29). A higher authority trumps them at that point.

Both Romans 13 and Hebrews 13 give us insight into the importance of understanding and obeying the authorities God has placed in our lives.

> Everyone must submit himself to the governing authorities, for there is no authority except that which God has established. The authorities that exist have been established by God. Consequently, he who rebels against the authority is rebelling against what God has instituted, and those who do so will bring judgment on themselves. (Romans 13:1–2 NIV)

> Obey your leaders and submit to their authority. They keep watch over you as men who must give an account. Obey them so that their work will be a joy, not a burden, for that would be of no advantage to you. (Hebrews 13:17–18)

Notice that Scripture does not tell us to

obey them only if we agree with their judgment. It simply says to "submit" to authority, and that whoever rebels is not rebelling against an individual but against God Himself.

So if a person in authority is misusing his position, you can know that he will be required to "give an account" for his own actions to an authority higher than himself. He is *more* accountable to God because he must answer to Him not only for his own performance but also for his leadership of those under him. That's a sobering thought — one that anyone in a position of authority should constantly remember.

Handling and responding to authority is serious business.

In fact, a biblical approach doesn't merely mean not showing disrespect to your authorities. You should actually *want* your leaders to succeed. You should be eager to help them fulfill their roles capably — your employers, pastors, law enforcement, elected officials. You will be to them like a rare breath of fresh air. Helping them to win actually sets you up to win their ear and gain their favor. Then if they make unwise decisions, respectfully appeal to them and pray for them, but maintain an attitude of Christlike honor even when you disagree

(1 Timothy 2:1–4).

This is how we should treat those over us — with a clear conscience, in respectful ways — not only from a fear of God but as a witness and an example to our children. Our kids will most likely adopt our views on authority in their own lives as well. Whatever patterns we set for them will be the ones they use to train their own kids and so on.

Like everything else in life, authority must be seen through a biblical worldview. We fail both ourselves and our children when we react on feelings alone, when we run at the mouth instead of trusting God and running back to His Word for wisdom, guidance, and direction.

We are His creation. We are accountable to Him — both to love Him and to fear Him. Our lives, therefore, are not about our plans, desires, and opinions. We are not here for our own pleasure and preferences but to please God alone. Our families will degrade if we do not bring things like our attitude toward authority under the *supreme* authority of His Word and His purposes for us.

When you teach your children to honor authority, you are teaching them to better honor God. Consider what you're modeling to your children in the area of honoring authority:

- When you're at home, how do you talk about your leaders at work and church?
- What do your children hear you saying about the government or elected representatives? Even if you disagree with them, is your attitude respectful?
- Do they see you praying for your authorities? (1 Timothy 2:1–4)
- How do they see you respond to speed limits and state troopers?
- Does this match your talk about how God places authorities in our lives for our benefit?

It has been said that what parents allow in moderation, their children will do in excess. So every generation of fathers must "be careful, and watch yourselves closely so that you do not forget the things your eyes have seen or let them slip from your heart as long as you live. Teach them to your children and to their children after them" (Deuteronomy 4:9 NIV), helping them not "forget his deeds" but to "keep his commands" (Psalm 78:7 NIV).

So obey the authorities in your life as unto the Lord. And teach your kids to do the same — as unto the Lord. It will help them obey *you.* If you don't train them to respect authority, and then they in turn quit respecting you, you will lose your influence and everything that goes with it. Honoring authority is a hallmark of godly men and their children.

But how do you instill honor into your children? How do you train them to respect your authority as a parent, as well as that of other leaders?

DISCIPLES AND DISCIPLINE

A major part of your role as a father is to *disciple* your kids, to teach them the ways of God and the realities of life from a mature, experienced, biblical perspective.

But *discipling* your kids requires *discipline.*

Discipline helps our children realize that sin is not only dishonoring to *God* and dishonoring to *us,* but it is harmful to *them.* As the book of Proverbs and Deuteronomy 30 reiterates again and again, the right choice is the smart one (the path to blessing), and the wrong choice is the stupid one (the path to punishment).

And discipline is what brings this point home for kids. It gives a clear, negative connotation to sin's costly consequences.

Therefore discipline doesn't feel good, nor should it. "No discipline seems pleasant at the time, but painful. Later on, however, it produces a harvest of righteousness and peace for those who have been trained by it" (Hebrews 12:11 NIV).

Discipline should be more on the father's shoulders than the mother's because of who we represent. Our loving discipline prepares our kids to respect and obey their heavenly Father.

> "We had earthly fathers to discipline us, and we respected them; shall we not much rather be subject to the Father of spirits, and live? For they disciplined us for a short time as seemed best to them, but He disciplines us for our good, so that we may share His holiness."
> (Hebrews 12:9–10)

So a father's job is to take the long view, not the short one. Discipline withheld may seem momentarily pleasant to the child and the parent. But many fathers — even good men like Eli in the Old Testament, the wise, priestly mentor to the young prophet Samuel — are failing to heed God's warning not to "withhold discipline from a child" (Proverbs 23:13). God said of Eli, "I have told him that I am about to judge his house forever for the iniquity *which he knew,* because his sons brought a curse on themselves and *he did not rebuke them*" (1 Samuel 3:13).

It takes no skill or courage to be a passive father — not when he knows that by failing to correct sin in his children, he is actually *encouraging* it. More than that, he is likely guaranteeing that uncorrected sin will follow his child into adulthood and follow his family into the coming generations. What takes *courage* is to faithfully and fairly dispense parental discipline — despite its momentary discomfort — knowing that sin will harm a child in far worse ways than even the painful discipline of a loving father. "He who spares his rod hates his son, but he who loves him disciplines him promptly" (Proverbs 13:24 NKJV).

Our children — just like us — are sinners living in a fallen world. And if we don't correct our own sinful tendencies as well as those of our children, each of us will stray further away from God's instructions and be left to live with the terrible consequences.

Scripture portrays a clear pattern: "Train up a child in the way he should go; even when he is old he will not depart from it" (Proverbs 22:6 ESV).

He'll walk right into the blessing of God.

God has designed obedience and honor to

be blessed with a full life and an easier yoke. That's why He says:

Children, obey your parents in the Lord, for this is right. "Honor your father and mother" — which is the first commandment with a promise — "that it may go well with you and that you may enjoy long life on the earth." (Ephesians 6:1–3)

It is a lie from the Enemy to believe that rebelling against and dishonoring authority brings more freedom and peace. Rather, Scripture says to "bring them up in the training and instruction of the Lord" (Ephesians 6:4). When we do, God will begin using their own consciences to convict them of a standard they know to be right and true.

Correction builds character.

Training leads to honor.

So at its heart, discipline springs from long-range love — a father's consistent promise to help correct his children and lead them toward a lifetime of blessing and responsibility.

DISCIPLINE IN ACTION

Now let's get practical: the level of discipline that a parent should give will differ depending upon the crime. Children that do something out of ignorance should receive more mercy and teaching than discipline. But when they know better and still rebel, the consequences should be greater.

If your child has intentionally done something worthy of receiving discipline, then you are the primary one responsible to make sure it is carried out. And the most effective way is to follow biblical principles. There are many forms of discipline, but God's Word communicates that a father should not be afraid to lovingly spank his children, especially in their younger years. Physical discipline is mentioned numerous times in Scripture, and God has approved of it as an instrument of justice and cleansing. Note these verses from Proverbs:

Foolishness is bound up in the heart of a child; the rod of correction will drive it far from him. (Proverbs 22:15 NKJV)

The rod and reproof give wisdom, but a child who gets his own way brings shame to his mother. . . . Correct your son, and he will give you comfort; he will give delight to your heart. (Proverbs 29:15, 17)

A loving spanking doesn't warp a child; it humbles them and helps them behave. Our culture may frown on the spanking of children. But the culture is not your authority — *God is.* And His Word says it's better that they experience the brief physical sting of a spanking for a few seconds than to grow up without an understanding of consequences throughout their lives. Our prisons are full of men and women who would trade their punishment for a child's spanking any day. If children learn to talk their way out of receiving discipline by crying, negotiating, or manipulating, they will learn to do it all the more as an adult.

And the more they do it, the less they will respect you or any other authority — the less *honorable* they will become. Ultimately this "fearless" view of authority will damage their image of God, the righteous Judge, who will not tolerate negotiating or manipulation on Judgment Day. By not disciplining them, we do our children a disservice by indirectly teaching them to dishonor God.

For physical discipline, the "rod" actually means a reed-like item for spanking, not a large weapon that could cause bodily injury. You should never strike your children in the

face or head, and never with a closed fist —
on *any* part of their body — which would
amount to child abuse. Instead a spanking
is most appropriately applied to their rear
end. A spanking should cause enough of a
short sting to get the job done but never to
wound a child physically or emotionally
long-term. Discipline is not intended for a
child's "destruction" (Proverbs 19:18) but
rather for his or her good. It's ultimately an
act of love.

But a father should not discipline his child
whenever he is in a rage or displaying
uncontrolled anger. If you're extremely
angry, send your child to another room until
you can calm yourself down. Don't discipline until you're emotionally under control.
Your kids should always know that when
you discipline them, your desire is to lovingly help them learn right from wrong, to
help them make better decisions in the
future, not to harm them.

Always clarify first with your child exactly
what happened and why any potential
discipline may be necessary. Help them see
their situation from God's perspective, not
just yours. If you choose to spank them,
then leave the room afterward for a few
minutes, and let them have time to cry
privately and think about what they've

done. Take this time yourself to pray for God to give them wisdom and a repentant heart.

After a few minutes, go back in and embrace them and comfort them. Tenderly remind them again why you needed to discipline them. Explain that you only want what's best for them, that you are accountable to God to train them, and that you love them very much. Tell them you are an imperfect father who makes mistakes of your own — that you're trying to do what is right, but you need God's mercy and forgiveness too, just like they do. Then pray with them, asking God to help them in the future to maintain a clean heart.

That's correcting a child with love. That's growing character to match their growing minds and bodies. That's looking down the road and seeing a destination worth the discipline. It's how children become men and women who honor authority and will hopefully one day fear God.

"I WILL TRAIN THEM TO LIVE RESPONSIBLY"

In the end, not only does discipline instill in children a biblical respect for authority, it also develops them into people who know they're responsible for their actions —

people who "own" their consequences. People who can be trusted with great responsibility.

So even as they grow — even when discipline begins taking the form of withheld privileges and freedoms rather than enforced spanking — we must stay diligent to help them see that irresponsibility never stops coming at a cost, no matter how old they get. They can't be blaming other people or passing the buck. They can't keep coming to us to bail them out of tight situations they've gotten themselves into. If they need to apologize or make restitution, they must own it. If a tough consequence comes to them as a result of their actions or decisions, they must own it.

Yes, there are times for lots of grace and mercy on the part of a parent. But this should always be considered in light of the status of your child's heart. God resists the proud and gives grace to the humble. If you can see they are learning to own up to their mistakes and showing sincere remorse for their actions, then wisely demonstrating extra grace may often be the best thing to help them grow.

Your decision to show mercy could help them see that God understands we can't always live up to His standard, that He doesn't take pleasure in punishment but in restoration and redemption. However, if your child is only trying to escape more consequences and is showing little genuine remorse, then discipline may be more appropriate. And the more you have your child's heart, the more effective you will be.

Our culture doesn't need any more kids who are good at skirting the system and getting away with as much as they can. We're raising children of honor. Children of responsibility. Children who know that if they make the mess, they clean it up. If they borrow it, they give it back in good condition. If they break it, they pay for it. If they make a promise, they keep it. Children who are a blessing to us and to others wherever they go. Who are strong leaders of families, businesses, churches, and governments of the next generation. Who love God, fear Him, walk in honor, and learn to let their light so shine before men that they may see their good works and glorify their Father in heaven (Matthew 5:16).

That's the kind of men we want to be. And that's the kind of kids we must grow and develop through our faithful example, training them to love God and to fear God, discipling them with a real-life understanding of their own sinful nature and sin's inescapably harmful consequences.

"Your kids honoring authority and living responsibly."

"Your kids changing the world for good and for God's glory!"

You've got to love the sound of that.

This is worthy of your resolution.

COURAGEOUS CHALLENGE

Ask your children if you have hurt them in any way in the past and never made it right. If so, apologize.

MEMORY VERSE

The conclusion, when all has been heard, is: fear God and keep His commandments, because this applies to every person. For God will bring every act to judgment, everything which is hidden, whether it is good or evil.
(Ecclesiastes 12:13–14)

He has showed you, O man, what is good. And what does the LORD require of you? To act justly and to love mercy and to walk humbly with your God.

Micah 6:8 (NIV)

CHAPTER 9
RESOLVE TO FIGHT
FOR JUSTICE

I WILL confront evil, pursue justice, and love mercy.

Every generation encounters evils that need to be confronted and addressed. And every generation needs strong men to rise up courageously against them.

This generation — for the sake of future generations — needs *you*.

Our culture — even many *Christians* in our culture — are slowly becoming numb to evils that twist and confuse our moral compasses. Men are tolerating more and more what God has said in His Word we should hate and despise. Not only are we failing to guard our hearts from moral filth and pollution, we are often entertained by the very things we should be regarding as wicked and shameful. Instead of grieving over the serious ills in our society, we have allowed ourselves to slip into sports and media-induced comas, oblivious to the real problems and issues that could use our attention. Instead of investing ourselves in efforts that could shape society for generations to come, we've crammed our schedules so full with work and entertainment that we don't have time for anything more substantial and eternal. The average American watches five hours of shows on television or over the Internet every day. That's the equivalent to non-stop viewing twenty-four hours a day for more than two months straight — every year. That time is usually noninteractive for families too.

How can we expect to hate evil if we routinely welcome it into our homes through the television and the computer screen? How can we impact our communities for Christ if we don't take the time to really care about them? How can we hope to play a role in influencing culture if we don't have time to notice and reach out to those who are suffering under its worst injustices?

The Scripture lays out three requirements that any man of resolution should take seriously to heart:

He has showed you, O man, what is good. And what does the LORD require

of you? To act justly and to love mercy
and to walk humbly with your God.
(Micah 6:8 NIV)

"To act justly" — to deal fairly and honestly with others, to confront evil both in ourselves and our society, and to intervene on behalf of the weak, vulnerable, mistreated, and oppressed.

"To love mercy" — to discern the physical and spiritual needs of others, and to represent the hands and heart of Christ to people who desperately need help, compassion, and deliverance from evil and injustice.

"To walk humbly with your God" — to live a circumspect and selfless life before Him, devoted to Him and to His Word, exercising our faith and love in a way that actively, consistently honors Him and His lordship.

Justice. Mercy. Humility.

The daily battle with evil.

Any time a man gets serious about loving God and loving his neighbor, it will always lead him out of his comfort zone and to a place where he must get his hands dirty confronting evil and bringing about justice while extending mercy. These are the things Jesus died for, and they are worth taking a personal stand for. They are higher causes rooted in love that are worth a man's sacrifice of money, convenience, popularity, anonymity, and even his so-called personal rights and entitlements. They are also tests of character that define the kind of footprint men will leave on this generation — the battles their sons and daughters will see them fighting for the cause of Christ, and then will take up themselves as they meet their own generational challenges with the same deep convictions.

Will you be that kind of man?

Will you be that kind of father?

Men resolved to be courageous don't shy away from the struggle. They know they were made to fight for what's right, and they're willing to strap the truth on and head into the battle. Even when it's hard.

Sometimes *very* hard.

"I WILL CONFRONT EVIL"

Men are wired by God to fight for what is right. When William Carey, "the father of modern missions," went to India in the late 1700s to tell them about the love and truth of Jesus, he was shocked to discover horrible atrocities among the Hindus — female infanticide, widows being burned or buried alive with their dead husbands, the sick and the weak being discarded like unwanted garbage. India's British government —

though aware of all this — didn't want to interfere or create a disturbance among people they didn't really understand. They found it easier and less troubling just to turn a blind eye to it.

But Carey, out of his compassion and love for the people, began writing against these practices in his missionary magazine and setting up public debates to air the issues and call for justice. He opened his home to children and the elderly who were left alone to die. He appealed to leaders in his English homeland, working for reform and legal remedies. He made many personal sacrifices — and made many personal enemies — but within his lifetime he was asked to translate into the Bengali language a decree from the British government that abolished many of these cruel customs. Carey had gone to India to share the gospel, and God used him to impact a culture by living what the gospel proclaimed.

Carey wasn't alone. Missionaries and evangelists like John Wesley actively opposed slavery. Charles Finney had a major role in the illegal Underground Railroad, saving the lives of many slaves while being criticized by fellow Christians because of his civil disobedience. D. L. Moody opened homes for underprivileged girls, rescuing them from exploitation. Charles Spurgeon built homes to help care for elderly women and rescue orphans from the streets of London. All of these were men who carried out the Great Commission for a living. But their evangelism was made most effective because they actually lived and practiced the gospel they preached.

As far back as Bible times, we see men taking hard stands for righteousness, truth, and justice.

- The prophet Nathan courageously confronted King David about his adulterous relationship with Bathsheba. (2 Samuel 12:7–9)
- Nehemiah spoke out against those who took financial advantage of others, who were forcing people into debt and slavery. (Nehemiah 5:6–13)
- John the Baptist eventually lost his head for publicly condemning King Herod's adultery and marriage to his own brother's wife. (Mark 6:17–18)
- When God's temple was being compromised through corrupt profiteering, Jesus upended the moneychangers' tables and drove them from the premises. (Matthew 21:12–13)

After Martin Luther posted his ninety-five theses in response to widespread corruption in the church of his day, he was hauled before the religious leadership in 1521 — as well as the Emperor himself, the highest civil authority — and was ordered to repudiate his "errors." Luther replied, "My conscience is captive to the Word of God. I cannot and I will not recant anything, for to go against conscience is neither right nor safe. God help me. Amen. Here I stand, I cannot do otherwise."[12]

British parliamentarian William Wilberforce, shortly after his conversion to Christ in 1784, began his battle for the black man's freedom. In the face of apathy, scorn, and strong-armed opposition from the slave industry, this one man relentlessly kept reintroducing to Parliament a motion for the abolition of slavery, vowing, "Never, never will we desist till we . . . extinguish every trace of this bloody traffic, of which our posterity, looking back to the history of these enlightened times will scarce believe that it . . . has been suffered to exist so long a disgrace and dishonor to this country." He died in 1833 — three days after the Bill for the Abolition of Slavery brought the unjust practice in England to its final end.

Twenty-seven-year-old Dietrich Bonhoeffer, even while many in Germany were celebrating Hitler's ascent to power, broadcast a message entitled "Christ Is Our Führer," preaching against the wicked leader for making an idol of himself and his office. Halfway through his message, the Gestapo cut off the transmission. But Bonhoeffer refused to remain passive while his countrymen were being murdered. As a leader in the German resistance, he was eventually captured and detained by the Nazis, then executed by orders of Heinrich Himmler, acting on Hitler's behalf. Had he been silent, he could have survived the war. But he was fighting in another war, serving another Commander. Stripped naked, Bonhoeffer was led to the gallows. The author of *The Cost of Discipleship* would pay the price he had written about: "When Jesus calls a man, he bids him come and die."

The disciple and the Führer both died in April 1945 — Bonhoeffer on the ninth, Hitler on the thirtieth. Exactly three weeks apart, both men faced God. Dietrich Bonhoeffer knew that a moment after his death, he would hear his Lord say, "Well done, my good and faithful servant." Adolf Hitler, a moment after his death, no doubt heard something terrifyingly different.

Martin Luther King Jr. saw social evils

with unusual insight and faced them with uncommon courage. He was a strong warrior against racial discrimination in 1950s and '60s America. Resisting the calls of many to lead a violent, bloody resistance toward the bastions of societal injustice, he championed a stronger, silent form of retaliation based largely on Jesus' teachings from the Sermon on the Mount. Such passive, nonviolent rebellion shocked a nation's prejudices by sheer numbers and stoic restraint. Many would be beaten and bloodied for taking bold stands of defiance. King himself would be shot dead as the inspirational leader of the movement. But as he had boldly stated, "Cowardice asks the question: is it safe? Expediency asks the question: is it politic? Vanity asks the question: is it popular? But conscience asks the question: is it right? And there comes a time when one must take a position that is neither safe, nor politic, nor popular — but one must take it simply because it is right."[13]

History is filled with examples of those who stood against the tides of injustice and immorality — men who courageously applied God's Word and His principles to situations where the Creator's purposes had been debased for personal gain or a thirst for power and cruelty. But our confrontation of evil and pursuit of justice should originate in our own homes, churches, and neighborhoods. Whether it's teaching our older children not to belittle the younger ones, confronting an alcoholic relative who's been beating his wife, speaking up for a coworker who's being trampled at work, or standing against unjust practices in our cities, we need to respectfully defend those within our reach who are being mistreated, taken advantage of, or led astray.

It's easy to look back years later and know these historical figures were right to counteract the wrongs that existed in their generation. But it's not always easy to know what actions to take now — when we're living in the midst of crisis. Only the man who relies on God and trusts in the timeless insights of His Word will understand what should be done . . . and done now.

The rights and future liberties of our children and grandchildren depend on what we are willing to sacrifice in our day on their behalf, because one generation's apathy and cowardice can squander and erase what the sweat and blood of previous generations have secured.

Will you live out the love of God that you profess? Will you open your eyes to the true needs around you? Will you seek God's will for this hour of darkness? Will you find the one thing He may be calling you to confront, and then commit yourself to leading and partnering with those who share your godly concern?

That's what men of resolution do.

They become the heroes of today. And tomorrow.

"I WILL PURSUE JUSTICE"

The recent church history in America includes a lot of good men doing nothing. Men who are wired, called, and empowered to be men of action, yet who choose to be soft, insensitive, and passive — men who fail to remember that "to one who knows the right thing to do and does not do it, to him it is sin" (James 4:17). Passivity is a curse.

Being a Christian once meant faithfully and boldly representing Christ, even when it came at great risk, even when it meant being unpopular. But too many men today have redefined being *Christlike* to mean "nice and quiet."

By that definition, however, even *Christ* wasn't always Christlike. He was known to confront people with their sin, sometimes raise His voice in righteous anger — even call people names to describe their blind indifference to God and to people's needs. If we don't challenge ungodliness and indecency in our culture, in government, in the entertainment media, and especially in the church, then we're trying to be *nicer* than Jesus.

Following Christ is counter-cultural. Most people won't encourage you to take stands that step on people's toes or upset the status quo. Fellow believers may even be offended if they see your position as being too radical or your cause too controversial. But in a world where people are passive and lenient in their opinions, swayed by prevailing agendas, tolerant toward sinful permissiveness, and consumed by selfish desires, you shouldn't expect much company when you choose to confront evil or care about the unlovely.

Yet whether it's acceptable to our tastes or not, men are called by God to love the world (the people for whom Christ died) in the way He loves it, and to *hate* the world (its sin and rebellion against Him) in the way He hates it. "Whoever wishes to be a friend of the world makes himself an enemy of God" (James 4:4).

"To act justly."

"To love mercy."

"To walk humbly."

To be courageous. We are to do this not only when it's convenient but also when it's costly. Not for others' approval but for the affirming "well done" of God's approval. Paul defended his own boldness in ministry by asking, "Am I now trying to win the approval of man, or of God? Or am I trying to please men? If I were still trying to please men, I would not be a servant of Christ" (Galatians 1:10 NIV).

We have an obligation before God to leave for future generations a society that is not riddled with injustice and immorality. This starts in our homes, where we set godly standards and shepherd our children underneath them. It extends to our churches, where we must avoid caving to the popular myth that the best way to reach the world is to become more *like* the world. Then our fight must go into other areas where public opinions are being shaped and cultural norms defined. Many Christians recognize that the ultimate solutions to our nation's problems are not political and judicial. But that's no excuse for being disengaged and passive in these arenas. Martin Luther King Jr. said, "Morality cannot be legislated, but behavior can be regulated. Judicial decrees may not change the heart, but they can restrain the heartless."[14]

We *can* influence people, including nonbelievers, on matters of justice and human decency. In the process we can tell them about Christ and show them the full implications of Christian truth and compassion.

Court decisions are gradually eroding religious liberties, usually with very little objection from God's people. Wherever Christians fail to stand up for what is right, our children and grandchildren will one day pay the painful price.

Will our grandchildren look back and wonder why we looked away and did nothing while rights were freely taken from us that men in past generations fought and died for? Will they be ashamed of our failure to stand up and speak out? These are legitimate questions. But they pale in comparison to the larger question: How will *Christ* evaluate our actions when we stand before Him at the judgment seat? (Romans 14:10–12; 1 Corinthians 3:12–15; 2 Corinthians 5:10).

A wise quotation attributed to Martin Luther expresses well a challenge for pastors and all Christian men:

If I profess with the loudest voice and clearest exposition every portion of the truth of God except precisely that point which the world and the devil are at that moment attacking, I am not confessing Christ. Where the battle rages, there the loyalty of the soldier is proven, and to be steady on all the battle fronts besides is mere flight and disgrace if he flinches at that point.

If you're only going to fight the battle in one place, fight it in your heart; if in two places, fight it in your heart and in your home. But realize you are also a steward of your church, community, city, state, and country.

We're at war — a spiritual battle against unseen but very real enemies. "We are not fighting against flesh-and-blood enemies, but against evil rulers and authorities of the unseen world, against mighty powers in this dark world, and against evil spirits in the heavenly places" (Ephesians 6:12 NLT). There is no end to the evil and destruction they will lead people into if not resisted. With this in mind, we should adopt godly lifestyles and make sacrifices so we may win the war. "Greater is He who is in you [Christ] than he who is in the world [the Devil]" (1 John 4:4).

We are called as men to resist the devil

wherever he seeks to destroy lives, steal human dignity, or suppress the cause of righteousness on earth. We can't do everything, but we can probably do much more than we're currently doing — not to make a name for ourselves but to magnify the name of Christ in our world.

"I WILL LOVE MERCY"

In the Great Commission — Christ's parting words to His followers before He returned to heaven — Jesus not only told His disciples to evangelize, He also told them to teach new converts "to observe all that I have commanded you" (Matthew 28:20). And among the many things Jesus "commanded" of us is the priority of being compassionate and taking sacrificial action for the weak and needy. If we fail to do this, we fail to fulfill the Great Commission.

Loving God cannot be separated from loving our neighbor (Matthew 22:34–40). When responding to a man who wished to define "neighbor" in a way that excluded certain groups of people, Christ presented the Good Samaritan as a model for what our behavior should look like (Luke 10:25–37), a man who went out of his way to help a victim lying in the ditch. The religious hypocrites looked the other way because they had more "spiritual" things to do.

Helping the poor has always set Christians apart, showing the world that we operate on a radically different value system. Sometimes it seems the church's highest value is what Francis Schaeffer called "personal peace and affluence." We want to be rich, comfortable, and at ease. We want to be accepted. We don't want to be inconvenienced or controversial. Above all, we don't want to suffer. But again and again, God's Word exhorts us:

> Defend the cause of the weak and fatherless; maintain the rights of the poor and oppressed. Rescue the weak and needy; deliver them from the hand of the wicked. (Psalm 82:3–4 NIV)

> Feed the hungry and help those in trouble. Then your light will shine out from the darkness, and the darkness around you will be as bright as noon. (Isaiah 58:10 NLT)

It is time for Christian men to stand up and do what is right, regardless of the cost or the change of plans in our lifestyle. This doesn't mean feeling guilty that God has entrusted us with abundance. We should be grateful to Him for that. But we should also feel very responsible to use the abundance He has given to help the less fortunate around us.

It's the courageous, compassionate, Christlike thing to do.

We should ask ourselves, "If Christ were on the other side of the street, or the city, or even the world, and He were hungry, thirsty, helpless, abused, or imprisoned for His faith, would we care enough to go help Him?" For we must not forget what Christ Himself said in Matthew 25:40. What we do to help the least of these our brothers, we do for Him. He *is* in our neighborhood, community, city, and country. He is everywhere in the world, awaiting the ministry of His people to the needy and persecuted people of our day. We are His hands and feet.

Will our children and grandchildren see us fulfilling this part of our *Resolution* calling? Will we show them that true success — the real pursuit of true lovers of God — is marked by extending that same love to the hurting, disenfranchised, lonely, and forgotten around us?

ALL FOR JESUS

There are many people in our world — not just Christians — who stand up against injustice. But believers in Christ have the greatest reason and motivation of all for confronting evil and extending mercy. Our purpose in fighting the good fight in our generation is to glorify the name of Christ, to serve others for His fame and renown. And because this is His desire, He promises the empowerment of His Spirit to help us persevere through the battle — no matter how hard, no matter how disrespected, no matter how far-reaching and sacrificial.

If Martin Luther King Jr., William Wilberforce, John Wesley, John the Baptist, or Dietrich Bonhoeffer were alive today, would they see the same injustices and evils we see and run ahead of us into battle? If they did, would we join them, or perhaps even race ahead of them? Or would we watch like cowards from behind the tall grass?

If our lives are centered on being against abortion, pornography, homosexuality, or sex trafficking — any single issue like that isn't enough. Certainly we should hate abuse in all its forms. God calls upon us to defend the poor and needy. But some people hate evil more than they love good. While love strengthens us for the long haul, hatred has a way of embittering us and burning us out. That should not be our drive! Paul said, "The love of Christ compels us" (2 Corinthians 5:14 NKJV).

To endure in a cause, we must make sure it's really about Jesus and His kingdom, and then keep reminding ourselves of His words: "Truly I say to you, to the extent that you did it to one of these brothers of Mine, even the least of them, you did it to Me" (Matthew 25:40). We need to lovingly reach out to those blinded and bound by evil. We are to follow Christ from start to finish.

If you wish to persevere, yield to the Holy Spirit and ask God to empower you. Then start moving your feet. Don't be shocked by opposition; be prepared for it. Many of us have forgotten what our forefathers knew — that adversity and persecution is normal for Christians. So sharpen your sword and prepare for the long march.

Charles Spurgeon, a nineteenth century British pastor who stood steadfastly against the evils of his day, said:

Fearless of all consequences, you must do the right. You will need the courage of a lion unhesitatingly to pursue a course which shall turn your best friend into your fiercest foe; but for the love of Jesus you must thus be courageous. For the truth's sake, to hazard reputation and affection is such a deed that to do it constantly you will need a degree of moral principle which only the Spirit of God can work in you; yet turn not your back like a coward, but play the man. Follow right manfully in your Master's steps, for he has traversed this rough way before you.[15]

God can use our courageous acts of justice and mercy to change people one at a time — and to change our families one generation at a time. When we lock shields and work together to pray fearlessly, to live the truth in love, to resist evil, to boldly speak up for those who cannot speak for themselves, we shine as lights in our darkened world. Many will not welcome our message, but many will. Let's not allow those who refuse the truth to stop us from proclaiming it to those who will be set free by it, because we know God will change our character and that of our children through our faithfulness to Him.

Jesus will be clearly seen and proclaimed.

The gospel will shine forth like the dawn.
And our strong Father will be well pleased.

COURAGEOUS CHALLENGE

Contact your local police department or youth detention center and ask them what the biggest concerns are in your city. Then pray for God to raise up strong men to help confront those specific issues.

MEMORY VERSE

He has showed you, O man, what is good. And what does the LORD require of you? To act justly and to love mercy and to walk humbly with your God. (Micah 6:8 NIV)

As those who have been chosen of God,
holy and beloved, put on a heart of
compassion, kindness, humility,
gentleness and patience.

Colossians 3:12

CHAPTER 10
RESOLVE TO DEMONSTRATE LOVE

I WILL pray for others and treat them with kindness, respect, and compassion.

Truth and justice must always be balanced out with love, kindness, and compassion. But a lot of us men think of love and kindness as a women's sport. Sure, we generally get past some of our inhibitions and are able to hug people on occasion — as long as it's short and doesn't call our manhood into question. We may not mind being tender at home with our families when no one else is watching. But the burden of being overly kind, or thoughtful and sensitive to others' needs, or called upon to offer comfort to someone — we freely delegate those jobs to our wives or mothers. Love is just not known as our strong suit.

We've got better things to do than worry about your feelings. You'll get over it.

In contrast, what most men don't realize

about love is that the strongest, manliest man of all time was also the most loving Man ever to walk the earth. Jesus Christ, the greatest Warrior for justice, went out of His way to show kindness, compassion, and respect to people from all walks of life. He reached out to the lowly fishermen as well as the prideful tax collectors. He spent time teaching the ignorant, ministering to diseased beggars, and giving His full attention to "irritating" children. He ate with sinners who disagreed with His teaching and who probably assumed He was a little deluded. There was no one He didn't treat properly, even when He rebuked the Pharisees with harsh truth that embarrassed them. He knew when to show both tender love and tough love, both to His friends and His enemies, but it was *love* just the same. He knew when to encourage His disciples and when to reprimand them. He died for all, not just those who loved Him. He was the perfect example of living a life of selfless love toward others. And He is our model to follow.

So for men who know they're a little deficient in the love department, but who realize they suffer from relationships that are shallow, disloyal, or sometimes awkward and uncomfortable, Christian love is the answer that can enrich their lives with greater meaning and purpose. We should never shy away from what is considered the most powerful motivation of all. Love is like rocket fuel that emboldens a man to serve his family, sacrifice for his neighbor, and lay down his life for a friend. It makes us turn from our naturally selfish bent and become increasingly more kind and compassionate.

But how do we develop a deeper capacity for kindness and compassion? Where do we start in our demonstration of it?

Well, the practice of *prayer* is the perfect place where love for others can really begin.

"I WILL PRAY FOR OTHERS"

Most Christian men would probably admit they don't pray enough. Unless there's a crisis or an important issue at hand, many would say that their prayers are limited to mealtimes, bedtime, and silently during church services — if that! But this weak record is not the mark of a courageous follower of Christ, a man challenged by God's call to love his neighbor as himself.

Only in Christ do we find the wisdom, strength, and motivation to accomplish what God has given us to do. Our kindness, respect, and compassion will never be driven by any natural, inborn tendencies of ours — not consistently. Until we devote ourselves to spending time with God in prayer, we will never get past the distractions of our day or the limitations in our love tank.

Prayer is our lifeline to spiritual health. To a man in need of God, it becomes as necessary as breathing. Inside the freedom of prayer, you can open up with God about your marriage and family issues, your friends and their needs, even your enemies and your responses to them. If it is worth worrying about, it is worth praying about.

Prayer can open your mind and tune you into what truly matters to God and the needs of the people around you. As you pray, God can change your heart and improve the way you think and relate to others and their needs each day.

So "pray in the Spirit on all occasions with all kinds of prayers and requests" (Ephesians 6:18 NIV). If you don't respect your pastor and want a better one, start praying for the one you already have. Pray "that God may open a door for [their] message, so that [they] may proclaim the mystery of Christ" (Colossians 4:3 NIV). If you don't feel much more than a passing wave of compassion for people who are suffering through hard times, then start praying for those who are "in trouble" or "sick" (James 5:13–14 NIV).

Committing to prayer is vitally important. You need it. God wants it. And it is a foolish man who chooses not to utilize it as a weapon in the battles of life — praying on his own behalf as well as others'.

But sometimes when we pray, we get no response — which can get frustrating. We start wondering if prayer works or God cares. So we quit praying and go back to trying to figure out life the best we can in our own strength.

But the Bible reveals that not only does prayer powerfully work, we must learn how to work prayer. There are some specific things that may be locking up your prayers and making the whole experience ineffective — things you can diagnose and deal with — as well as some important keys to transforming prayer into a daily, ongoing adventure with God.

Here they are:

The Ten Locks That Make Our Prayers Ineffective

1. *Praying without knowing God through faith in Christ.* Jesus said, "I am the way, and the truth, and the life; no one comes to the Father but through Me" (John 14:6). If a

man hasn't been saved and surrendered to Christ as Lord, he has no mediator between himself and God and is unwelcome in the holy of holies (1 Timothy 2:5).

2. *Praying with an unrepentant heart.* The psalmist realized, "If I had cherished sin in my heart, the LORD would not have listened; but God has surely listened and heard my voice in prayer" (Psalm 66:18–19 NIV). Clinging to sin and stiff-arming God makes God stiff-arm us. If you hold on to sin and refuse to confess it, you cannot take full hold on God.

3. *Praying for show.* "When you pray," Jesus taught, "you are not to be like the hypocrites; for they love to stand and pray in the synagogues and on the street corners so that they may be seen by men. Truly I say to you, they have their reward in full" (Matthew 6:5). Prayers can be made in public, but only sincere hearts connect with God.

4. *Praying repetitive, empty words.* Why do we think God wants to hear canned, lifeless, unthinking prayers? Jesus said, "When you are praying, do not use meaningless repetition as the Gentiles do, for they suppose that they will be heard for their many words. So do not be like them; for your Father knows what you need before you ask

Him" (Matthew 6:7–8).

5. *Prayers not prayed.* "You do not have because you do not ask" (James 4:2). It seems obvious, but one of the reasons our prayers don't get answered is because we never got around to praying them.

6. *Praying with a lustful heart.* "You ask and do not receive, because you ask with wrong motives, so that you may spend it on your pleasures" (James 4:3). God isn't fooled by prayers that are more about how we can fulfill our sinful desires than how we can honor Him and fulfill His purposes.

7. *Praying while mistreating your spouse.* "Live with your wives in an understanding way . . . and show her honor as a fellow heir of the grace of life, so that your prayers will not be hindered" (1 Peter 3:7). If you don't listen to your wife, then God won't listen to you.

8. *Praying while ignoring the poor.* "He who shuts his ear to the cry of the poor will also cry himself and not be answered" (Proverbs 21:13). If we do not cultivate a generous, compassionate heart, we become spiritually impoverished and God ignores us.

9. *Praying with bitterness toward another.* Jesus said, "Whenever you stand praying, forgive, if you have anything against anyone, so that your Father who is in heaven will

also forgive you your transgressions. But if you do not forgive, neither will your Father who is in heaven forgive your transgressions" (Mark 11:25–26). Unforgiveness indicates a closed, resistant heart in us, which closes off our prayer life as well.

10. *Praying with a faithless heart.* The man who wants to hear from God "must ask in faith without any doubting, for the one who doubts is like the surf of the sea, driven and tossed by the wind. For that man ought not to expect that he will receive anything from the Lord, being a double-minded man, unstable in all his ways" (James 1:6–8). If we don't really believe He cares or can, then He says He won't.

The Ten Keys That Enable Prayer to Be Effective

1. *Praying by asking, seeking, and knocking.* Jesus said, "Ask, and it will be given to you; seek, and you will find; knock, and it will be opened to you. For everyone who asks receives, and he who seeks finds, and to him who knocks it will be opened. . . . If you then, being evil, know how to give good gifts to your children, how much more will your Father who is in heaven give what is good to those who ask Him!" (Matthew 7:7–8, 11). We should be specific and persis-

tent and keep praying until something happens.

2. *Praying in faith.* "All things for which you pray and ask," Jesus said, "believe that you have received them, and they will be granted you" (Mark 11:24). When followers of Christ believe He can and will, then He likely will . . . in His way and in His timing. He invites us to be bold enough to ask for big things.

3. *Praying in secret.* Jesus also taught that "when you pray, go into your inner room, close your door and pray to your Father who is in secret, and your Father who sees what is done in secret will reward you" (Matthew 6:6). When we pray alone, God knows it is more sincere and not for show. Seek to be close to Him even when no one's watching.

4. *Praying according to God's will.* "This is the confidence which we have before Him, that, if we ask anything according to His will, He hears us" (1 John 5:14). When we pray for what God wants more than what we want, He will answer us. You can ask for whatever you want, but you should trust His response since He knows what you really want and need better than you do.

5. *Praying in Jesus' name.* "Whatever you ask in My name, that will I do, so that the

Father may be glorified in the Son. If you ask Me anything in My name, I will do it" (John 14:13–14). When we know Christ, we pray based upon His name, His reputation, His authority, and His track record, not our own worthiness. We don't earn God's ear, but Jesus already has it. Every time our heavenly Father answers us, He is glorified through what Jesus has done.

6. *Praying in agreement with other believers.* Jesus said, "If two of you agree on earth about anything that they may ask, it shall be done for them by My Father who is in heaven. For where two or three have gathered together in My name, I am there in their midst" (Matthew 18:19–20). United prayer works. To agree means to make a harmonious symphony. We pray in different ways, but we intercede together for the same beautiful result.

7. *Praying while fasting.* Paul's pattern was that after they had "appointed elders for them in every church, having prayed with fasting, they commended them to the Lord in whom they had believed" (Acts 14:23). After Esther's people fasted and prayed, they had a major breakthrough. Come with a heart that's hungry and thirsty for God instead.

8. *Praying from an obedient life.* "If our

heart does not condemn us, we have confidence before God; and whatever we ask we receive from Him, because we keep His commandments and do the things that are pleasing in His sight" (1 John 3:21–22). An obedient heart is unashamed and at home in His presence, not afraid of being found out, not holding anything back.

9. *Praying while abiding in Christ and His Word.* "If you abide in Me," Jesus said, "and My words abide in you, ask whatever you wish, and it will be done for you" (John 15:7). Praying while staying in close fellowship with Him and His Word sets us up to pray much more effectively. His Word renews our minds and lines up our prayers with His heart and mind.

10. *Praying while delighting in the Lord.* "Delight yourself in the LORD; and He will give you the desires of your heart" (Psalm 37:4). The word *desires* means "petitions." When we are satisfied with Him alone, He feels free to give us things we wanted to pursue but didn't.

You can summarize all the locks and keys of prayer this way: if you will get right with God, get right with other people, and then get your heart right, you can get busy praying and watch God work in amazing ways. The bottom line is that "the earnest prayer of a righteous person has great power and produces wonderful results" (James 5:16 NLT).

In prayer you can become a very dangerous man. For good.

The Bible says that God wants us to have freedom and confidence when we pray (Ephesians 3:12). This means nothing is holding us back *from* praying and nothing is holding us back *while* praying. No guilt, no doubt, no fear, and no hindrance. When we pray, we are not talking to an impersonal, careless God but to a loving Father. So we just need to be patient and trust His heart that He is doing what is best for us and for His greatest glory.

Then as we learn to pray more effectively, we will realize that one of the kindest actions we can do for others is to pray for them. To intercede on their behalf and seek His involvement in their lives is both compassionate and Christlike. If someone has ever told you they're praying for you, it is very encouraging.

Prayer doesn't just "change things." It changes *us.* Relating to God with new openness and consistency gives you not only a desire but also the ability to become a different "kind" of man — one who learns to treat others with true love and respect.

"I WILL TREAT OTHERS WITH KINDNESS, RESPECT, AND COMPASSION"

When Jesus was asked to boil down all of God's commandments to their essential ingredients, He said that no commandments were greater than loving God with all that we are and loving our neighbor as ourselves (Matthew 22:36–40).

This raises a question for us. If the second greatest commandment of all is to love our *neighbors* (which is a general reference to all the people around us), then do our "neighbors" see a difference in us they don't see in non-Christians? Are we demonstrating the kind of love that Jesus says we should be expressing toward others?

What would it look like if we did?

First, His love isn't always soft and gentle. Love doesn't mean being a pushover, someone that others can walk on because they know we won't do anything about it. To truly love a neighbor means to do what's best for them and help them get on right terms with God (or *stay* on right terms with God). And as we all know, this often calls for some straight talk and courageous conversation. In addition to serving, sacrificing, and going the extra mile, love means getting tough when necessary to show how much we really care about others.

Jesus was gentle and kind, but when Peter took Him aside, telling Him that he would never allow his Master to be killed on his watch, Jesus rebuked him: "Get behind Me, Satan; for you are not setting your mind on God's interests, but man's" (Mark 8:33). Jesus' decisions would come from aligning His actions and expectations with God's will, not Peter's desires. It took a sharp word from Jesus to get that through to him.

But that's love. That's caring more about what someone else needs than about what they want or whether they like you or not. Most men don't have the guts to do this. Demonstrating love often means doing something hard and uncomfortable if it's what's best for a friend.

Second, His love helps you love people who are not like you. What difference does it make if the only people you choose to favor or be around are those who look like you, act like you, and agree with your religious and political views? How are you expanding the reach of God's kingdom by keeping your attention contained to a tight, limited circle of like-minded friends?

Loving others as Jesus loved them means recognizing everyone as being a creation of God. The Bible says God made us in His image, so when we devalue others in our minds because of their race, color, gender, or social status, it's the same as telling God that He could've done a better job of making them. In contrast, Scripture says to "regard one another as *more important* than yourselves" (Philippians 2:3). If Jesus could humble Himself to take on human flesh, walk in our shoes, and even give Himself to die on the cross for our sins, then who are we to judge others because they don't have our education, financial status, or abilities?

The Samaritan woman that Jesus met at the well was the opposite of Him in every way, but He still reached out to her in love and kindness (John 4:7–26). To put His love in today's terms, it's like a wealthy, heterosexual boss from America reaching out in compassion to his hurting coworker who may be a homosexual female maintenance worker from another country.

Our love should know no bounds. Christ was a friend to sinners, died for all, and still shows no favoritism. That includes people of any nationality, any body type, any background, and any personality style. We are all sinners in need of His grace. And we should extend that grace freely to others He places in our paths.

"So, as those who have been chosen of

God, holy and beloved, put on a heart of compassion, kindness, humility, gentleness and patience" (Colossians 3:12) — not just for people you tend to like but those who are probably the most in need of somebody to love them in Christ.

Third, His love makes you respectful. When Jesus presented truth to unbelievers, He left it up to them as to how to respond. He didn't force it down their throats. He didn't twist their arms to make them follow Him. He spoke the truth with love and grace while showing respect. Though rebuking or challenging a brother in the faith can often be the most loving way to treat him, our behavior toward those who do not believe should be graced with extra warmth, compassion, and kindness. This is the most effective way to reach them.

As Paul said, "The Lord's bond-servant must not be quarrelsome, but be kind to all, able to teach, patient when wronged, with gentleness correcting those who are in opposition, if perhaps God may grant them repentance leading to the knowledge of the truth, and they may come to their senses and escape from the snare of the devil" (2 Timothy 2:24–26).

Don't take judgment into your own hands. Put yourself in their shoes. Show love toward those who don't recognize the Word of God as the standard to live by. Why would they adhere to rules they don't believe? If they are spiritually blind (2 Corinthians 4:4), spiritually dead (Ephesians 2:1), and a slave to sin (John 8:34), why would we expect them to think or act like a Christian? Instead let your compassion demonstrate the God you serve and the Savior you worship. Expressing genuine love can crush the doubts of the skeptic and open the heart of the hardened prisoner. Let your heart for Christ be seen in how you treat them. If they are your coworker, relative, or neighbor, don't be surprised if God gives them a great need and sets you up to meet it. Or a crisis where you can show compassion. This is the environment where truth takes root — where we "overcome evil with good" (Romans 12:21).

Are you known for loving others? Do your children see you as a man who respects everyone and shows compassion for the hurting? Would they say you love your neighbor as yourself?

Remember, your example will likely be adopted by your kids. If they see you acting with consistent kindness and compassion toward people around you, they'll catch the desire and confidence to do the same thing. As you pray with them for opportunities to show love and share their faith, you will celebrate together how God works through you as a team.

Which brings us back to the importance of prayer. You may not have put a lot of thought into loving the people in your life or the strangers on the corner. But in prayer, God can draw out of you His own love for others. He can tweak the consciences of those you know and meet, making them unexpectedly hungry for a relationship with your God. And He can turn you loose with a new freedom to care about them — something that honestly wasn't there before.

A coach looks for players to put in the game who are physically ready, mentally focused, and who know the plays. If you resolve to be prayerful, respectful, and loving toward others, God will give you more opportunities for ministry than you can imagine, making your life a real source of Christlike blessing and joy to people's hearts — for God's glory and praise.

Let's start praying about that.

COURAGEOUS CHALLENGE

Write a letter of appreciation to your father or pastor.

MEMORY VERSE

As those who have been chosen of God, holy and beloved, put on a heart of compassion, kindness, humility, gentleness and patience.
(Colossians 3:12)

Lazy people want much but get little, but those who work hard will prosper. . . . Work brings profit, but mere talk leads to poverty.
Proverbs 13:4; 14:23 (NLT)

CHAPTER 11
RESOLVE TO PROVIDE FOR YOUR FAMILY

I WILL work diligently to provide for the needs of my family.

Blessed are the breadwinners. As men, we should consider it an honor to embrace our role as the primary providers of our families. This is part of our manhood and calling as representatives of God the Father — the One who established work as part of His creation and is *still* "working" (John 5:17) as an example for us to follow, continually providing for our daily needs.

We could significantly reduce the poverty level in our country if every father who had checked out on his wife and kids would go home and start taking his role as provider seriously. "I will work diligently to provide for the needs of my family" is a desperately needed resolution that every man called "father" should boldly make. The word *father* means "source," among other things.

Jesus said that when we need something, we should pray and ask our "Father who is in heaven" to provide it for us (Matthew 7:11).

Psalm 23, the most famous chapter of comfort from the Bible, is also a vivid picture of a loving shepherd providing for the flocks under his care: "The LORD is my shepherd, I shall not want" (verse 1). Starting from that opening statement, this psalm describes how God not only provides us with food, water, and rest but also meets our emotional and spiritual needs as well. "He restores my soul" (verse 3). Bottom line, if we have a legitimate need, then God our Father is on it. Even when the path seems dark and difficult, He is there, watching over us, comforting us, and taking care of us.

And for men — "shepherds" over our families — few things make us feel stronger and more masculine than knowing our wife and kids could say the same of us. "My dad is my shepherd, and I don't lack anything I need."

While many wives sacrificially help their families financially (Proverbs 31:16–24), husbands should always see themselves as the primary providers as shepherds over their homes. No, we can't give our families everything they want or everything we wish we could. But by God's grace, operating through our hard work, they don't have to worry if their needs will be met.

"My husband is a great provider."

Love hearing that.

Some men, struggling to find good-paying work, may feel like failures for not being able to temporarily fulfill their desire to provide financially. In tight economies, in down seasons, God often allows families to go through lean times, testing their faith and discovering where their trust and priorities really are.

These are the dark moments when courageous husbands and fathers must battle through their insecurities, fears, and feelings of desperation to continue offering the provisional leadership their families need, even as they scrimp and save. God knows what is in a man's heart, and He will not fail to provide opportunities for us to physically care for our families as we seek Him. His promise to His children is that "God will supply all your needs according to His riches in glory in Christ Jesus" (Philippians 4:19).

For others, however, this resolution comes with a grave warning: "If anyone does not provide for his own, and especially for those of his household, he has denied the faith and is worse than an unbeliever" (1 Timothy 5:8). Some men are not providing for their families because they're not willing to

269

put in that much hard work and sacrifice. But a change of heart could ignite the motivation that pulls his family back from the brink of destruction. A man of lazy habits, transformed by God into a man of labor and faithfulness, can change the course of his family for generations.

That's the raw power of God's provision.

WE WORK, GOD PROVIDES

Work is a wonderful thing. Even though part of the consequence of sin is that work now involves "painful toil," "thorns and thistles," and "the sweat of your brow" (Genesis 3:17–19 NIV), the diligent worker is honored throughout Scripture, and the lazy man is not.

Poor is he who works with a negligent hand, but the hand of the diligent makes rich. (Proverbs 10:4)

He who steals must steal no longer; but rather he must labor, performing with his own hands what is good, so that he will have something to share with one who has need. (Ephesians 4:28)

For you yourselves know how you ought to follow our example. We were not idle when we were with you, nor did we eat anyone's food without paying for it. On the contrary, we worked night and day, laboring and toiling so that we would not be a burden to any of you. . . . For even when we were with you, we gave you this rule: "If a man will not work, he shall not eat." (2 Thessalonians 3:7–8, 10 NIV)

In cultures that offer welfare or subsidized income to the unemployed, a man without a job may be forced to temporarily accept this as a way to fulfill his obligations to his family. But when work becomes available to him, an honorable man will choose to earn his food and provide for his own household. This trait separates the diligent man from the lazy man. Laziness, theft, and gambling are all sinful and dishonorable ways to try to get things you want without really earning them. These are never God's plan.

Even if it means doing menial work for a while until a better job opens up, *any* work to a diligent man is preferable to him than sitting around, dodging opportunities, and waiting for his ship to come in.

Men work. Men provide. And when those men are children of God who call on Him as their Father, they can be sure that God will always meet their needs. They will eventually be able to say as King David did,

"I have been young and now I am old, yet I have not seen the righteous forsaken or his descendants begging bread" (Psalm 37:25). God Himself will honor the work we do because He is a "rewarder of those who seek Him" (Hebrews 11:6).

When we get prayerfully busy trying to provide for our families, we find ourselves cooperating with the One who created it all, owns it all, and can make more of it whenever He wants. By laying our best before Him, we can be absolutely sure that He will "give us each day our daily bread" (Luke 11:3). He is *Jehovah-jireh* — the God who provides.

After thousands of years of faithfulness, He will not ruin His reputation on us.

One thing we need to acknowledge soberly is that God does not promise to provide for the needs of those who are not His children. He may, but He is not obligated to do so. When Jesus promised God's faithful provision, He was talking about those who called God their Father (Matthew 6:25–34). Those who have rejected God or are worshipping false gods may starve (Deuteronomy 28:15–48; Isaiah 8:19–22; 65:12–13). Their gods do nothing for them. This is another reason why it is vital to tell them about the living God who owns the cattle on a thousand hills and can fill the hungry soul with what is good (Psalm 107:9).

However, Jesus taught believers to pray in confidence because "your Father knows what you need before you ask Him" (Matthew 6:8). Christian men who worry at night about their job or not having their needs met do so in vain.

The question for believers is never, "Will God provide?" but "How is He going to do it?"

God provides in His own way and in His own timing, but He is always faithful to His role as Provider. If you need transportation to get to work, God may provide a car to you free of charge as a gift from someone. Or He may provide the money to buy the car. Or a way to earn the money to buy the car. Or send you a bicycle. Or change your job so you can walk to work or even work from home.

But you can rest assured that He is on it and in the end will deliver what you need so you can get food on the table. And in the meantime, you need to walk by faith and stay busy asking, seeking, and knocking until He reveals what He has provided. But He will; you can rest on it.

The Bible is filled with amazing stories of how God provided His children exactly *what* they needed, exactly *when* they needed it. Sometimes He waited until the very last second, but He timed things perfectly to maximize His glory and maintain His reputation.

And that's what we can expect from Him, too, as we're obedient to pursue our calling as men who work hard to provide for our families and resist any temptation toward laziness.

MOTIVATION AT WORK

For some men, however, the "working hard" part is not the problem. Truth is, they're working *too* hard and *too* much — because their work is not motivated by the right things.

Some men are driven by fear. It's easy to get so wrapped up in the cause of providing that you become fearful you may not be able to make enough, and you start looking to money and work as your god. Jesus warned His followers not to let worry slip into our lives:

> "Look at the birds of the air, that they do not sow, nor reap nor gather into barns, and yet your heavenly Father feeds them. Are you not worth much more than they?" (Matthew 6:26).

If you are seeking Christ and His kingdom above all, He will make sure you never fail to have your basic needs met. Never.

Some men are driven by greed. Our goal in working can go far beyond provision and responsibility into materialism and covetousness. Instead of working for our families, we're working for better stuff, bigger awards, or recognition that we don't need. Instead of trying not to live in *want,* we just want more.

But if a man is not grateful for what God provides through reasonable, honest work, he will never be happy no matter how much he works and earns and accumulates. "He who loves money will not be satisfied with money, nor he who loves abundance with its income. This too is vanity. When good things increase, those who consume them increase" (Ecclesiastes 5:10–11). Many claim that they aren't making it financially, but what they really mean is that they lack the money to keep up with their appetites. They reach for a standard of living out of their reach. Or they eat more, buy more, accumulate more, and are entertained more than they should. Or they are impatient and rush into needless debts instead of waiting for purchases. Then they must work more to keep up with their creditors.

And this just never stops.

And so neither do they.

The resolution to provide for your family actually comes with a companion resolution: *to accept contentment,* not allowing yourself to fall in love with money and advancement and competition with others. It's a man with an "evil eye" who "hastens after wealth," the Bible says, not knowing that "want will come upon him" (Proverbs 22:28). Therefore, "if we have food and covering, with these we shall be content" (1 Timothy 6:8).

And here's why, as Paul went on to say:

Those who want to get rich fall into temptation and a snare and many foolish and harmful desires which plunge men into ruin and destruction. For the love of money is a root of all sorts of evil, and some by longing for it have wandered away from the faith and pierced themselves with many griefs.
(1 Timothy 6:9–10)

Clearly the Bible does not say it's a sin to be rich. But to love money — to *long* to be rich — eventually brings a lot of unnecessary stress, pain, dissatisfaction, and worry into our families. We cannot serve God and

276

money at the same time (Matthew 6:24), and we cannot take anything with us into eternity except deeds that please the Lord. Working for status or selfish gain is bad business.

After all, once your obligations are filled, God's design for your work is not to line your pockets with profits. He tells you to honor Him with your tithes and offerings (Malachi 3:10), to share with others who are in need (Ephesians 4:28), and to help further the work of the gospel with the fruit of your labor (1 Corinthians 9:14). In addition, the context of 1 Timothy 5:8, which speaks of providing for your "household," includes taking responsibility for others outside your immediate nuclear family, such as your widowed mom or grandmother who is without a husband to care for her. The motivation to work can never be greed but love — love that motivates you to go the extra mile, to use His provision to bless those around you and advance His kingdom cause.

Therefore, think of any extra income you receive from your work as being temporary and available for God's use — in whatever way He directs you to dispense it. It's noble to save for the future, but don't hold it too tightly, for it already belongs to Him and is ultimately meant for His glory.

Your motivation to work is actually a test of who you are serving. If you are serving money, you can expect to feel anger and frustration anytime things don't go as planned. But if you are working "as unto the Lord and not unto men" (Ephesians 6:7), then you will have greater joy, and even menial jobs will become fulfilling. You can then honor the Lord and reach worthwhile, spiritual goals no matter the status of your job or income.

SPIRITUAL AND EMOTIONAL PROVISION

Another danger for men to avoid — besides the twin extremes of laziness and overwork — is the belief that financial provision is the extent of your responsibility as a husband and father. Bringing home a paycheck and keeping your family clothed and fed are not where provision stops. As the shepherd-leader of your home, you're also responsible for providing spiritual and emotional sustenance for your family to feed on.

We've looked already at what it means to be the spiritual head of your home, but it cannot be emphasized enough that a child's primary view of God begins with his view of his earthly father. This is why it's so crucial that every father resolve to prioritize the spiritual health of his home — not only by maintaining his personal walk with God, not only by praying and reading the Bible with his family, but also by orienting his work schedule (as much as possible) to make sure he has the time, brain cells, and margin to keep his spiritual goals for his family protected.

You must stay active in church, for example, rather than letting work continually interfere with your regular involvement. Scripture tells us not to "give up meeting together, as some are in the habit of doing" (Hebrews 10:25). Making the Sabbath a day for worship, rest, and family togetherness, rather than just another day for working and catching up, helps you keep "first things first" with God and at home — and keeps your working life in healthy balance. Taking Sundays off prevents burnout and actually sharpens you to get much more done at work in less time.

But in addition to spiritual matters, providing for your family's *emotional* needs must also remain a priority. One reason to avoid constantly coming home drained and depleted from too many hours of work is so you're not as likely to be touchy, impatient, and irritable around your family. Part of their emotional well-being depends on the pleasantness of your conversation, your ability to give them your full attention, and your quickness to be understanding and forgiving.

Your children need to keep seeing that they're still important to you. They need to feel confident that other, less crucial concerns won't routinely and repeatedly take their place.

And don't fall for the logic that says you can make up for a lack of time with your family by appeasing them with gifts. This should be done sparingly — and only when your separation from them is necessary. Gifts are certainly thoughtful and can demonstrate love, but they are no match for your personal time and attention. Anything we give our children is a poor substitute for ourselves.

The term *affluenza* was coined to describe the unhealthy tendency of busy parents to smother their children with pricey possessions. This saturation of gifts leaves an extremely materialistic mind-set in children, who grow up constantly expecting freebies they haven't worked for. This ungrateful attitude breeds a laziness and self-centeredness that leads to a lack of responsibility as well as depression and anxiety.

Make time for them instead, and teach them the necessities of life. Model for them how to keep work in its rightful place. Your children will not remember what you did *for* them as much as what you did *with* them. And the example you set will likely be the path they display for their kids.

Too many Christian men love their wives and children, yet they overwork to be able to afford a beautiful house, expensive pleasures, and enough money for the children to go to college. Their children grow up with plenty of material things but without their father at home. Don't let your work — even the noble ideals of being a good provider — steal you away from your family so that you fail them spiritually and emotionally at home. If it means not taking a promotion, not winning an award, or making less money in order to spend needed time together, then do it. Many men need to pray for a new boss or a new job. But they should not keep sacrificing their lives and families for people who won't cry at their funeral.

Men never lie on their deathbeds and wish they could have spent more time in the office. They always long to go back and spend more time with their wife and kids. If you prioritize God's priorities, He can give you greater favor at work, bless you in ways your job never could, and stretch out the income you do bring in.

WHAT PROVIDING LOOKS LIKE

If you want to find out how you're doing as a provider in your home, why not ask your kids? "Do you feel like your needs are met? How can I do a better job of taking care of you? What makes you feel safest and most secure? Are you confident that I love you and will always be there for you?"

This also applies to your marriage. You don't have to read twelve books to learn what wives need from their husbands. Just walk up and ask her. If she doesn't have an answer, or if you have to pick her up off the floor, then tell her to think it over and make a list to share with you. *This is gutsy leadership on your part.* Your family feels things and thinks things about you anyway. You may as well know what they're thinking. Don't find out after it's too late.

When you take seriously your responsibility as a provider, you feel an inner joy that comes from pleasing God. In addition, your family will naturally grow in their respect and appreciation for you. This is just a by-product of dads doing what they're designed to do. If you're divorced, you need to make sure you're still providing for your ex-wife and kids. The fact that you are no longer married doesn't relieve you of responsibility for obeying God in these areas. If you've fallen behind in supporting your family, start praying about how you can sacrifice to catch up. Don't deny it or fight it. Just trust God and do it.

Circumstances are irrelevant when it comes to being a provider. Even in times of high unemployment and a poor economy, God expects us to fulfill our obligations, and He will help us to be found faithful if we will seek His help. Sometimes He will intentionally allow difficult financial circumstances to force us to our knees so He can turn them around as a platform to show us His power and love. But in every season, in every situation, and in every sense of the word, men of courage are men who *provide* for their families.

Resolve to provide well for yours!

COURAGEOUS CHALLENGE

Begin the practice of doing weekly family devotions.

MEMORY VERSE

My God will supply all your needs according to His riches in glory in Christ Jesus. (Philippians 4:19)

If you are presenting your offering at the altar, and there remember that your brother has something against you, leave your offering there before the altar and go; first be reconciled to your brother, and then come and present your offering.

Matthew 5:23–24

CHAPTER 12
RESOLVE TO RECONCILE WITH YOUR PAST

I WILL forgive those who have wronged me and reconcile with those I have wronged.

"How blessed is he whose transgression is forgiven, whose sin is covered!" (Psalm 31:1). If you want to see a happy person, look at someone who has just been forgiven! They have a refreshing humility and joy that's hard to deny. Regret doesn't have the power to haunt them anymore. They sinned or failed others, but they've been forgiven and set free. It's a beautiful thing!

But there's another joy worth pursuing — the liberation you feel after forgiving someone who has deeply hurt *you*. When wounded people finally forgive, the dark clouds part in their emotions, and a breath of fresh air and sunshine rushes into their hearts.

Bitterness can hold any good man down.

Guilt can turn the mightiest men into cowards. Both of these spiritual burdens result from failing to respond wisely to failure — *bitterness* from not forgiving those who have wronged you, and *guilt* from sinning against God and others . . . without making it right. But you cannot be a faithful man of resolution who walks closely with God unless you release the baggage from your past — both the bitterness *and* the guilt. If you don't, life will be like running a marathon with bricks in your pocket or driving your car with the parking brake on. Bitterness and guilt add unnecessary weight and waste our time and energy.

As men are embracing responsibility today, they must let go of yesterday. It's hard to have a vision for what's ahead when you're constantly haunted by what's in your rearview mirror. That's why God is passionate about reconciliation and is in the business of bringing good fruit out of rotten situations. We fail and He restores. We confess and He forgives. The entire Bible is an unfolding saga of how God is powerfully redeeming mankind to Himself.

Reconciliation — Past and Present

God is at perfect peace within Himself. God the Father, God the Son, and God the Holy Spirit are in complete unity within the Godhead. No bitterness, anger, guilt, or lack of harmony. Only intense love, joy, and peace. And each of us has been created in God's image, called to know Him and follow His example.

So as we pull up a seat to His table as a member of His family, we must line up our lives with the unity that is already in God, "being diligent to preserve the unity of the Spirit in the bond of peace" (Ephesians 4:3).

Yet we often sin, hurt others, and leave a trail of wounded lives behind us. When we withhold forgiveness for others' sin, we keep relationships broken that could thrive again. But reconciliation is so important to God, He sent Jesus "to reconcile all things to Himself, having made peace through the blood of His cross" (Colossians 1:20). Through our repentance and faith in Him, we are reconciled to God and forgiven fully of our sins. "Having been justified by faith, we have peace with God through our Lord Jesus Christ" (Romans 5:1).

His death brings reconciliation.

His grace brings peace.

And now, as recipients of this amazing redemption to become men miraculously living at peace with God, He calls us to join in the amazing work of helping others be reconciled to God as well. We are "ambassadors for Christ" (2 Corinthians 5:20), charged with declaring through our words and our lives that "God was in Christ reconciling the world to Himself, not counting their trespasses against them" (2 Corinthians 5:19).

But how do we best do that? And how do we do it *at all* unless we do the hard work of reconciling our own relationships with others — with our spouse, with our parents, with our children, with distant relatives, with discarded friends, even with bitter enemies?

We need to become experts at learning how to quickly work through issues. Courageous during conflict. Dead to ourselves. Hard to offend and quick to forgive. We must quickly humble ourselves and apologize when we stumble. An apology does not demonstrate weakness but incredible maturity and strength. We should never let pride get in the way of doing the right thing.

In order for us to do this, however, God needs us to be at a place where we have no hatred toward another person and no anger still festering in our hearts. Peacemakers at peace. No bitterness with anyone, and no one who has reason to stay bitter with us.

To be a reconciler is our calling as Christian men. To actually live it out calls for men of resolution.

EVERYDAY FORGIVENESS

The first part of this resolution is to fully embrace the power of forgiveness, to be sure that no "root of bitterness" has lodged in your heart against anyone (Hebrews 12:15). Is there anyone who has wronged you in the past that you have not fully forgiven? *Anyone?*

When we don't forgive, we throw other people into a debtor's prison inside our hearts. It's like we're saying, "You wronged me, so I'm going to stay angry with you until you pay for what you've done." But when Jesus was teaching His disciples how to pray mountain-moving, powerful prayers, He said, "Whenever you stand praying, forgive, if you have anything against anyone, so that your Father who is in heaven will also forgive you your transgressions" (Mark 11:25).

Did you see that? He said to forgive *"anything* against *anyone."* He wants absolutely *no* bitterness in us, nor does He want our obedience to be dependent upon someone else's. Others may or may not repent of what they've done, and we don't need to keep anger hanging in a holding pattern until they do. Sometimes your offender may already be dead, meaning you'll never get the apology you always wished you could hear. But God doesn't want their past sins holding you back in the present. He wants you to go ahead and forgive and let Him deal with them in His own wise way. It may seem wrong or unfair to forgive someone who doesn't deserve it and hasn't asked for it, but there are many vital reasons for doing so.

Strong relationships and marriages don't happen because people never hurt each other. They happen because the people involved keep on forgiving. It's impossible to go through life without getting hurt by someone at some point. Jesus said, "Offenses must come" (Matthew 18:7 NKJV). But God in His mercy has set up this amazing thing called forgiveness — the escape route for getting out of our own prisons of bitterness to restore broken relationships with others. We forgive not "up to seven times, but up to seventy times seven" (Matthew 18:22).

We must never stop forgiving. We may get

angry and then confront. But the very day we stop forgiving is the day we poison a relationship and ourselves. If we are not careful, one wrong can derail us.

God sees each day as its own unique package. At creation, for example, He finished each thing He did in a day. His Word says not to "worry about tomorrow; for tomorrow will care for itself. Each day has enough trouble of its own" (Matthew 6:34). Jesus' model prayer is a daily prayer: "Give us this day our daily bread" (Matthew 6:11).

So as we are praying to "our Father in heaven" each day, we are also asking Him to "forgive us our debts as we also have forgiven our debtors" (Matthew 6:12) — *every day.* When we refuse to do this on any given day, then both the guilt from our own sins as well as bitterness against others' sins begins to slither in like a snake and inject venom into our lives.

God's mercies are "new every morning" (Lamentations 3:23) — and so should ours be. He wants us to deal with our junk quickly, keep short accounts, and then move on. But when we go to bed angry and carry it into the next day, a bitter root springs up and grows in us — unfulfilled revenge that tries to punish another with our anger. Any time we close our days without clearing our emotional accounts, things turn sour.

Have you forgiven someone . . . today?

THE FRUIT OF UNFORGIVENESS

Many bitter fruits come from a bitter root. Ephesians 4:26–31 opens with the appeal not to "let the sun go down on your anger. Do not give the devil an opportunity."

Then it goes on to list the horrible things bitterness is able to produce in our lives.

Opportunities for the Devil (Ephesians 4:26–27). Jesus said the thief comes to "steal and kill and destroy" (John 10:10), and this is exactly what the Devil does in our lives when we give him a foothold. He tries to steal our faith and leave us with fear, steal our joy and leave us with depression, steal our love and leave us with hateful thoughts toward others. The name *Satan* means "accuser." And by accusing others in our minds, he causes us to dwell on their wrongs, filling in the unknowns with negative assumptions, keeping us focused on how we've been mistreated and unappreciated. He feeds us what we want to hear with one hand, then takes from us the peace that is rightly ours with the other.

Unwholesome speech (Ephesians 4:29). It doesn't matter what you're talking about; bitter people will bring up the person they are angry with and start verbally running them down. If you are talking to a bitter person, be careful that their venom against others doesn't poison you.

Grieving the Holy Spirit (Ephesians 4:30). Our anger grieves God's Spirit, not only producing bitter fruit but quenching the fruit of the Spirit in our lives. Rather than operating with love, joy, and peace toward others, a bitter person becomes hateful, negative, and restless, closing off his heart toward others. Bitter people become very unlike themselves. The most loving and joyful people in the world can become hateful, irrational pessimists if they let bitterness take root and don't forgive.

Believe it or not, bitterness even hurts us *physically.* "A joyful heart is good medicine, but a broken spirit dries up the bones" (Proverbs 17:22). The tension of trying to contain it can harden our facial features and make us lose the radiance of our countenance, even causing a chemical imbalance in our bodies and lowering our resistance to disease.

Emotionally, socially, and of course spiritually, bitterness depresses and contaminates us. It dries up our fellowship with God so we become like barren, deserted land. God feels far away. Our time in worship and in His Word becomes powerless and joyless. Our prayers feel weak and ineffective. Jesus said, "If you do not forgive others, then your Father will not forgive your transgressions" (Matthew 6:15).

It has been wisely said: "Bitterness does more damage in the life where it is *stored* than the one on whom it is *poured.*"

The clear conclusion to all of this is that we must *forgive!* If we are going to obey God and be like His Son — we must forgive. If we want to get the poison out of our lives and keep our marriages and relationships strong — we must forgive. If we don't teach our children to forgive, then they won't forgive us when we fail. If we want to help others walk in unity and love, we must set the example first ourselves. Or else.

"I WILL FORGIVE THOSE WHO HAVE WRONGED ME"

God alone is ultimately the judge over a person's sinful actions, not us. He alone knows their background, their baggage, and their upbringing. He alone knows the details concerning what they were thinking and what their motives were at the very moment they wronged us. More important, He alone knows the perfect judgment for that person, and He is the only One qualified to carry it out.

So when we get bitter, we are actually stepping into the place of God on the judgment seat. We are making assumptions as to what happened and why someone did something. Then we are determining to punish them ourselves — by throwing them in the prison of our angry hearts. But when we do, we don't really hurt that person at all. We only hurt ourselves further and bring truckloads of unwanted consequences into our lives. We are saying in essence, "To get you back for hurting me, I'm going to hurt myself even more!"

But a bitter heart doesn't see it that way. "If I forgive," some say, "it means that what they did to me was all right. If I forgive, they'll be getting away with the wrongs they've done to me."

Not true. The very fact that their offense requires your forgiveness indicates that what they did was wrong. That's the whole point. Forgiveness is pardoning a legitimate debt that is owed. Your forgiveness will not release them from the consequences of their sin. But it will release *you* from the burden, weight, and pain of having to worry about holding them accountable yourself for their sins. That's God's job. He's on it. And by forgiving, you get to heal and move on.

Nobody's saying this is easy. *It's not.* Pastors, psychologists, and counselors will tell you that getting someone to forgive is one of the most difficult challenges of all. Even after discovering the many reasons why forgiveness is so vital, some people still refuse to do it. Maybe one of those people is you.

"I've been hurt too deeply!" you may say. Well, was it worse than what your sin did to Jesus? Do you realize how deeply He suffered because of you? Yet He still forgives. The deeper the hurt, the more God will give you grace to help you handle it and stop the bitterness.

"I don't need to forgive. It happened too long ago. I've moved on." Then why do the angry emotions come back when you remember it? If you didn't consciously forgive, you may have just mowed over the weeds without pulling up bitterness by the roots.

"That person doesn't deserve my forgiveness!" You're right. No one does. Forgiveness is a gift. That's why one of the greatest demonstrations of God's love for us is that He completely forgives us even though we didn't earn it and don't deserve it.

"I just can't do it. I'm not able to forgive." Again, you're right. You can't do it without

God's help. But you can do all things through Christ who strengthens you (Philippians 4:13), and He is the One "who is at work in you, both to will and to work for His good pleasure" (Philippians 2:13), giving you the desire and power to do what is right. Forgiveness is something that comes from the heart of a merciful God. He designed it, extends it, and commands us to share it with others. "Be kind to one another, tenderhearted, forgiving each other, just as God in Christ also has forgiven you" (Ephesians 4:32).

So don't look for reasons why you shouldn't. Look for reasons why you should.

How do you forgive?

1. *Let it go.* Forgive the same way Jesus forgives: freely and willingly. Acknowledge God as the rightful Judge over that persons' life — the One who has told us, "Never take your own revenge, beloved, but leave room for the wrath of God, for it is written, 'Vengeance is Mine, I will repay,' says the Lord" (Romans 12:19).

2. *Give it up.* Ask God to forgive you for refusing to forgive those who have hurt you. Ask Him to cleanse and release you and to take back any ground or foothold the Devil has claimed in your heart.

3. *Just do it.* Forgive deeply "from your

heart" (Matthew 18:35). Face it head on, then prayerfully and intentionally tackle it. Choose to say, "I fully forgive them, God! I'm releasing them completely! I'm turning all the judgment, anger, and vengeance over to You!" And God, who knows exactly what happened, knows exactly what the issues are, and knows exactly how much wrath or mercy to show them, will provide all the vengeance necessary. But don't keep putting it off. What's stopping you from forgiving right now?

Forgiveness doesn't mean not confronting others about what they've done. You may still find it necessary and appropriate to go to that person and share what happened, trying to "show him his fault in private; if he listens to you, you have won your brother" (Matthew 18:15). You may need to wisely set up some boundaries and accountability to keep this person from doing it again — both for their good and yours. But regardless, you need to completely forgive on your end. Confront them as one who has already forgiven, not as a bitter judge.

Then finally, walk each day in perpetual forgiveness. You can forgive someone on Monday, think about the hurt again on Tuesday, go to bed angry on Wednesday, and be bitter by Thursday morning. So watch out!

When true forgiveness takes place, you'll begin to experience a clear breakthrough. You will feel a weight drop off your shoulders. The anger will turn to compassion. Instead of hating them, you will feel sorry for them and what they have done, but you won't still be angry about it. Your walk with the Lord and joy as a Christian will go to a fresh new level. Someone has said, "To forgive is to set a prisoner free . . . and discover that the prisoner was you." We don't lose anything when we forgive. We gain back our lives.

"I WILL RECONCILE WITH THOSE I HAVE WRONGED"

The second part of the forgiveness resolution — in addition to forgiving those who have wronged you — is to "reconcile with those I have wronged." Our natural tendency is to be so preoccupied with wrongs others have done against us, we then minimize, rationalize, and deny our sins against God. We become embittered at how He has allowed us to suffer at others' hands, rarely considering how others have suffered at ours.

But when you have mistreated another person or mishandled a relationship, you are the one causing them to go through all the pain and heartache we've been discussing so far in this chapter. *You* are the one leading *them* toward a pit of bitterness. Plus, your vertical relationship with God is directly affected by the unhealthy condition of your horizontal relationships with people you've offended.

That's why Jesus explained:

> If you are presenting your offering at the altar, and there remember that your brother has something against you, leave your offering there before the altar and go; first be reconciled to your brother, and then come and present your offering.
> (Matthew 6:23–24)

Regardless of how he or she receives your apology, you are still responsible to humbly apologize for anything you have done wrong.

"If possible," the apostle Paul said, "so far as it depends on you, be at peace with all men" (Romans 12:18). And this often means being willing to man up and confess the sins you've committed toward others.

Our defense mechanism is to resist this and to cover things up. There are three things we men do to conceal our sin. First, we deny or hide our involvement in something wrong. Then, if caught, we admit our actions but deny that it was wrong. Third, if we admit it was wrong, we then blame others for what we have done.

That's us. Sinful, human, self-centered, self-defensive men.

But regardless of our rationale, any refusal to confess the wrongs we've committed only displeases God and hurts us further. King David wrote:

> When I kept silent about my sin, my body wasted away through my groaning all day long. For day and night Your hand was heavy upon me; my vitality was drained away as with the fever heat of summer.
> (Psalm 32:3–4)

Any unconfessed sin will continue to trip us up and prevent us from moving forward in life. It causes situations to get more tangled and complex — only harder to unravel later on. "He who covers his sins will not prosper, but whoever confesses and forsakes them will have mercy" (Proverbs 28:13 NKJV).

You will never reconcile with your past by sweeping your own mistakes under the rug but by taking full responsibility for them.

When the tax collector Zacchaeus met Jesus Christ, the experience changed his life completely. His initial reaction was to go back and make things right with those he had wronged. He said, "Look, Lord! Here and now I give half of my possessions to the poor, and if I have cheated anybody out of anything, I will pay back four times the amount" (Luke 19:8 NIV). What a powerful apology! That's genuine, courageous faith!

Imagine if a government tax employee showed up at your door and said, "My life was changed through a relationship with Jesus Christ, and God has convicted me of how wrongly I mistreated you. I'm here today to apologize for what I've done and to pay back what I've cheated from you. Will you forgive me?" It would astound you.

So if Zacchaeus could travel through time and step into your shoes, to whom would he go and apologize on your behalf?

God begins to work in mighty ways when men humble themselves and do the right thing. Like Zacchaeus, we need to get things right with those we have wronged — financially, morally, emotionally, spiritually. Paying debts, making restitution, bringing healing. Why? Because we serve a mighty God who is worthy of our best. And we represent Him with our lives and our integrity. We cannot walk closely with Him and have anything to share with others until we have a clear conscience. We must get things right "before God and before men" (Acts 24:16). Not clearing our conscience can "shipwreck" our faith (1 Timothy 1:19).

The consequences of admitting failure and apologizing only last for a few minutes, but the benefits are lifelong and unending — freedom, joy, friendship, peace, integrity. Just plug the Golden Rule into your situation. Don't you wish the people who wronged you in the past would get right with God and apologize to you?

Keep these few things in mind as you go about mending the bridges you've burned:

First, pray beforehand for the humility, the words, and the favor of the other person. Pray for them to have compassion and mercy. If there is any insensitivity or pride in you, they will tend to resist your words.

Second, focus on their pain, and don't blame. Your apology is not about what guilt has done to you or what they have also done wrong. It's about what your sin has done to them. Others are more willing to forgive and move on if they know you have considered their pain a real offense.

Third, make it up to them. Giving some type of gift can be significant in communicating that you value them. "A gift given in secret soothes anger," the Bible says (Proverbs 21:14 NIV) — not in manipulating, but in letting the person see some tangible proof of your sorrow and desire not to do this again.

Most people receive an apology with mercy and open arms, but some are unresponsive. And you must be patient. They may need time to process what's just happened. They may need to see more of a track record from you before they're ready to rebuild trust. You cannot force another's forgiveness. But you can give them as much space and time as they need to respond, and you can stay close to God every day, asking Him to enable you to build a new, consistent pattern of faithfulness and honor.

God blesses those who hunger and thirst to be right with Him and with others. Relationships often become stronger than ever, in fact, after an apology and forgiveness have taken place. We as men must lead the way and show our families what it looks like to be bridge builders, wound healers, and relationship restorers. Our God is worthy of this! And life is too short not to do it.

Is there anyone who has hurt you that you need to forgive today? Then do so. Is there anyone from your past who can say you wronged them and never made it right? If so, start asking God to prepare the way and prepare their heart for you to square things.

Forgive. Release. Apologize. Repent. And "may the Lord of peace himself give you peace at all times and in every way. The Lord be with all of you" (2 Thessalonians 3:16).

COURAGEOUS CHALLENGE

Write out a list of names of those who have hurt you in the past, and forgive each of them just as Christ has forgiven you. Mark off their names one by one.

MEMORY VERSE

Never pay back evil for evil to anyone. Respect what is right in the sight of all men. If possible, so far as it depends on you, be at peace with all men.
(Romans 12:17–18)

Vindicate me, O LORD, for I have walked in my integrity. I have also trusted in the LORD; I shall not slip. Examine me, O LORD, and prove me; try my mind and my heart. For Your lovingkindness is before my eyes, and I have walked in Your truth.

Psalm 26:1–3 (NKJV)

Chapter 13
Resolve to Live with Integrity

I WILL learn from my mistakes, repent of my sins, and walk with integrity as a man answerable to God.

Failure is a powerful teacher. It's always better to learn from counsel or someone else's mistakes, but the reality is, we are all going to "stumble in many ways" throughout our lives (James 3:2). And how we respond when it happens is the real test, for those responses to failure will either make us stronger or further damage our relationship with others and with God.

A wise man learns quickly from his errors and adjusts his path to get back on track. He tries to *fail forward,* becoming wiser after each mistake and taking intentional steps to avoid stumbling into the same ditch twice. A foolish man, however, *fails backward,* refusing to learn, continually wasting his experiences. He follows his own footprints into yesterday's traps and gets entangled in them all over again. "Like a dog that returns to its vomit is a fool who repeats his folly" (Proverbs 26:11).

So if we are going to live with integrity, we must tune our ears to both the lessons of our own life and the wisdom of others. We must humble ourselves, admit we don't have it all together, and then ask God to give us wisdom each day to make the best decisions possible. When we do, He promises He will pour it on us "generously" and not make us feel foolish for asking (James 1:5).

Whether it's fighting off an unhealthy habit, seeking marriage counseling, or requesting direction concerning our finances, we should never be afraid to ask for help from others. Everyone needs it. And victory comes to those with many advisors (Proverbs 24:6).

When you look at your life, what do you see? Do you see a history of lessons learned or failures repeated? Do you see a man who listens to instruction or resists rebuke? We should develop the mind-set each time we fail that once is more than enough and then quickly adjust our course in order not to relive the wreckage.

"I WILL REPENT OF MY SINS"

One of the evidences of true Christians is their war against sin and their sincere repentance from it. Men who are living in perpetual repentance are the ones God uses with much greater spiritual effectiveness.

But where learning from mistakes requires a change of mind-set, repenting of sins requires a change of heart. All believers in Christ should become *master repenters.* We are naturally good at sinning, but we need to get even better at repenting.

Repentance is transformational. It can mark the difference between heaven or hell, joy or sorrow, victory or defeat.

To *repent* basically means to turn away from sin and turn back to God. From self-rule to Christ-rule. From darkness to light. It's putting God first in your life and removing anything that keeps you from walking intimately with Him. It's *conviction* leading to *confession,* which brings *cleansing* leading to *communion.*

It's a clear change of direction.

When God's prophets in the Old Testament showed up in a city, they called the people to repent. Nobody liked it, but everybody needed it — God's mercy packaged as a painful warning. Those who listened and turned back to God found great favor, grace, and blessing. But those who didn't repent watched God keep His promise to send the painful and often catastrophic wages of their sin.

Hundreds of years later, John the Baptist — and then Jesus after him — continued to preach the same message: "Repent, for the kingdom of heaven is at hand" (Matthew 4:17). And those who turned from their sin and turned to the Savior found salvation, healing, and peace with God.

This message has not changed. Believe it or not, until the judgment seat of Christ, God's call for men to "repent" (Revelation 2:5; 16:11) remains the message all men need to hear.

God is now declaring to men that all
people everywhere should repent,
because He has fixed a day in which He
will judge the world in righteousness.
(Acts 17:30–31)

Repentance is an incredible opportunity often misinterpreted as an inconvenient obstacle. On the front end, people fight repentance because it exposes the ugliness of their sin and forces them to deal with it. But on the back end, repentance leads to life, joy, and peace with God and others.

This hard pill to swallow is actually the very remedy we need for a sick soul.

Everything good you are wanting God to do in your life is on the other side of repentance. Repentance leads to breakthrough. It brings the prodigal home. It unlocks the restoration of marriages. It opens the windows and lets in fresh air. Repentance takes you from bondage to freedom. From hardheartedness to tenderness. Distance to intimacy. Languishing to love. It is a gift from God, and you should receive it with gratefulness. It's the Holy Spirit saying to you, "I love you. I want to answer your prayers and greatly use you. But before I do, we need to deal with this first."

This is the point when you either resist Him or agree with Him, when you find out just how badly you want Him to cleanse you from your sin and change you completely.

But why does God keep requiring this of us? Why must walking in repentance become such an ongoing practice for a follower of Christ? Why so much, and why so often?

It goes back to our misunderstanding of sin.

THE DNA OF SIN

If you were to look at sin under a microscope, you'd discover that at its cell level, sin is the rejection of God in our hearts. It is the denial of His character, authority, and control over our lives.

Lying is not wrong just because it ruins our trust but because God is truth and never lies. It is the betrayal of who He is. *Murder* not only stops a beating heart but is contrary to the One who is life and love and made us in His image. *Sexual immorality* is not wrong simply because it leads to heartache, unwanted pregnancy, and disease but because God is holy and calls us all to lovingly reflect His faithfulness and purity.

This is the real reason why sin falls short of bringing God the "glory" He is due (Romans 3:23). Instead of revealing the awesomeness of His attributes through our obedience, sin denies the very nature and beauty of God. The love of God is denied when a man cheats on his wife. The patience of God is rejected when a father is easily angered and verbally abuses his kids. Instead of living as though God is holy and the most important aspect of our lives, our sin communicates that He is actually not that important and should not be taken seriously . . . which is a lie. Every instance of murder, adultery, abuse, divorce, deceit, and theft can be tracked back to the presence of sin, where there should have been kindness, respect, patience, and love.

This is ultimately why sin has such major consequences. This is why "the wages of sin is death" (Romans 6:23). Sin can be pleasurable for a few minutes, but it leaves us with a long-term list of major problems:

- Spiritually — sin separates us from God and makes us His enemies (Colossians 1:21–22)
- Emotionally — sin brings anger, bitterness, fear, worry, and guilt (Proverbs 10:19–20)
- Morally — sin makes worthless things seem valuable in our lives, and vice versa (Proverbs 5:8–14)
- Personally — sin enslaves and destroys us (John 8:34)
- Ministerially — sin can disqualify us from effective service to God (1 Corinthians 9:27)
- Internally — sin poisons our hearts so we quit loving others (2 Timothy 3:2–4)
- Relationally — sin brings brokenness and pain to our relationships (Proverbs 14:34)

- Historically — sin caused the Son of God to die a brutal death for us (Romans 5:8)
- Eternally — sin offends God and makes us wholly unfit for heaven (Matthew 13:40–43)

Sometimes we tend to describe sin as only the big stuff — murder, rape, adultery, prostitution, homosexuality, or abortion. But sin is much more than that. *We are all sinners.* Sin includes our everyday struggles with pride, self-righteousness, greed, anger, bitterness, materialism, lust, and lies — even those times when we just don't do what we're supposed to do. We need to view sin — *all* sin, *our* sin — the way God views it. Foul. Dirty. Hateful. Dark. Unholy. Ungodly. Unclean. Filthy. Spiritual leprosy that must be cleansed.

When God calls us to repentance, He's not trying to make our lives harder than they already are. He is lovingly looking down on our pride, perversion, and resistance to obey, and seeing vile offenses that are utterly corrosive to us. He says, "Stop! Turn around and come to Me. Let Me meet your needs and satisfy you in ways your sin never can. Be set free from what's holding you back so you can move on to better, higher things!"

Then Satan gives us false warnings: Don't you realize God is trying to take away your fun?

But in response the Holy Spirit wields the sword of God's Word and reveals how He "richly supplies us with all things to enjoy" (1 Timothy 6:17). He shows us in creation that He is the maker of beauty, of friendships, of children's laughter, of the wonder of love — even of our capacity to enjoy each of these.

Satan retorts, "But God is trying to limit your freedom!" Yet the Devil fails to tell you that sin is actually what enslaves you. He doesn't want you to realize that "if the Son makes you free, you will be free indeed" (John 8:36), and that God's commands actually protect your freedom.

"God is trying to make your life boring!" he continues. But the voice of Jesus rises up and says, "I came that [you] may have life, and have it abundantly" (John 10:10).

"No, God is going to make you so unhappy!"

And the Word of God slashes back with, "The fruit of the Spirit is love, joy, and peace" (Galatians 5:22). It is at this point that you must decide whom you are going to trust and what you are going to do. You must choose.

"Do it later!" the Devil finally offers. But delay is only extended disobedience.

God's Word rises up in power and says, "Submit therefore to God. Resist the devil and he will flee from you. Draw near to God and He will draw near to you. Cleanse your hands, you sinners; and purify your hearts, you double-minded" (James 4:7–8).

That's the only way to deal with sin — to see it for the gross wretchedness it is and see God as the holy cure to your weakness and discouragement. To agree with God that what He says is wrong in His eyes is also wrong for you too.

"If we confess our sins, He is faithful and righteous to forgive us our sins and to cleanse us from all unrighteousness" (1 John 1:9). And when we do, He rushes peace and freedom into our hearts as the power of Christ not only removes our sins but the guilt too, setting us up for healing, freedom, and future service.

Repentance is a beautiful, violent assault on sin.

It puts Christ back in the driver's seat where He belongs.

TRULY REPENTANT

If you are not careful when dealing with repentance, however, you may only be doing it halfheartedly. Compare the confessions of King Saul (1 Samuel 15:10–35) and King David (2 Samuel 12:7–15; Psalm 51) to discover the vivid difference between false and true repentance.

- Saul only confessed what was exposed; David confessed completely.
- Saul blamed others for his mistakes; David took responsibility on himself.
- Saul misunderstood the consequences; David knew he had gotten what he deserved.
- Saul's regret resulted in disobedience; David's sincerity led to humble service.
- Saul's life ended in shame and tragedy; David's ended with glory and honor to God.

In the New Testament, we see Judas *betray* Jesus, and Peter *deny* Jesus. Yet their responses to these failures were completely different. Judas had a change of mind, while Peter had a change of heart. Judas *regretted* what he had done and went out and hanged himself. Peter *repented* from what he had done and lived the rest of his life in passionate obedience to God.

The apostle Paul wrote a great explanation of what true repentance looks like. He had written earlier to rebuke the Corinthian church for their immorality, telling them to repent. Then after learning of their obedient response, he wrote the following words in a follow-up letter:

I am not sorry that I sent that severe letter to you, though I was sorry at first, for I know it was painful to you for a little while. Now I am glad I sent it, not because it hurt you, but because the pain caused you to repent and change your ways. It was the kind of sorrow God wants his people to have, so you were not harmed by us in any way. For the kind of sorrow God wants us to experience leads us away from sin and results in salvation. There's no regret for that kind of sorrow. But worldly sorrow, which lacks repentance, results in spiritual death. Just see what this godly sorrow produced in you! Such earnestness, such concern to clear yourselves, such indignation, such alarm, such longing to see me, such zeal, and such a readiness to punish wrong. You showed that you have done everything

necessary to make things right.
(2 Corinthians 7:8–11 NLT)

"Everything necessary." Whatever it takes.

If you are humbled and broken by your sin, not making excuses or blaming others for what you have done — if you accept the consequences and are not angry with those disciplining you — if you are willing to do whatever it takes to be restored, and if there is long-term change in your thinking and behavior . . . then your repentance is real. You're back on track!

But if you confess only so you can feel better and look better — if you are angry about the consequences — if you don't think you'd have done anything differently if you could go back and do it over, and if you make no changes to keep from doing it again in the future, then your repentance is *not* real.

Regret and tears don't mean repentance; *change* does.

But maybe it's deep remorse that keeps you from repenting. You may feel like your wrongs are piled too high to even deal with — like you're about to be crushed under the weight of guilt that hangs over your heart every day. It's true that each of us is wicked to the core apart from Christ. Our hearts are "deceitful above all things" (Jeremiah 17:9 NIV), and "all our righteous acts are like filthy rags" (Isaiah 64:6 NIV).

But if God could forgive the apostle Paul for tormenting Christians, and if God could forgive King David for adultery and murder, He can forgive you. If God could restore Peter to service after he had lied and denied Jesus three times, then He can restore you.

"Therefore repent and return, so that your sins may be wiped away, in order that times of refreshing may come from the presence of the Lord" (Acts 3:19).

And to show you mean business, make some bold changes. Be willing to change unhealthy relationships, rearrange your routines, and throw out stumbling blocks. Set up better boundaries. Stronger accountability. Stay in close fellowship with God, who loves you and wants to fill you and lead you.

Any individual has the capacity to commit any sin if he gets out of fellowship with God long enough. Just look at King David. A man after God's own heart. Filled with God's power. Writer of psalms. Walking in wisdom. Intimate in worship. Yet over time, he slowly became prideful, let his guard down, and then committed great wickedness.

So we should daily rely on God's grace. Confessing our sins is not a one-time affair. It is a lifelong daily habit. When we blow it, we should quickly confess and turn away from it. We need to keep tender consciences before God. Not just today but for a lifetime.

A lifetime of integrity.

"I WILL WALK WITH INTEGRITY"

Integrity means "wholeness" or "completeness" — the opposite of *hypocrisy*. The Bible uses the terms "upright" or "blameless" to describe a man of integrity. He continually thinks, speaks, and walks honestly before God and others. Jesus rebuked religious hypocrites for their lack of integrity because they honored God with their lips but their hearts were far away from Him (Matthew 15:8).

If you are a man of integrity, then you will speak the truth *all the time,* whether generally in broad terms or specifically when reporting facts. Whether much is at stake or *nothing* is at stake, you will be the same in public as you are in private. When you're alone, working late, on the Internet, or filling out your tax return, you will consistently choose to do the right thing. You're not perfect, but you are committed to walking in truth.

There is a cry for integrity in our land. We desperately need men who will keep their word in leading our churches, our businesses, and our government. The Bible says that pastors and deacons must be "blameless" (1 Timothy 3:2, 10 NKJV). Leaders stand on their integrity. Proverbs 16:12 says, "It is an abomination for kings to commit wicked acts, for a throne is established on righteousness."

Integrity reflects God. There is no deceit in Him. No corruption. No darkness. John 3:33 says, "God is true," meaning He is exactly who He says He is. He's not hiding an evil dark side or misleading you in any way. There is no injustice or deceit in what He does. His *words* are true, His *ways* are true, and His *judgments* are true. And because He is looking for followers who will worship Him "in spirit and truth" (John 4:24), your job as a man of resolution is to embrace a life of truth and integrity before Him.

And when you do, He promises these incredible rewards:

- Blessings in your *heart* — the light of a clear conscience in your eyes. The confidence of knowing you don't have to be afraid of bad news or being found out (Psalm 37:37; 112:7).

- Blessings in your *home* — "The righteous man walks in his integrity: his children are blessed after him" (Proverbs 20:7 NKJV) and will be "mighty on earth" (Psalm 112:2).
- Blessings in your *city* — the influence of your dependability and honesty on the entire community around you (Proverbs 11:11).

Through your integrity, God promises you strength (Proverbs 10:29), guidance (Proverbs 11:3), defense from attack (Psalm 7:10), and deliverance from trouble (Proverbs 11:6). The man of integrity is a "delight" to the Lord (Proverbs 11:20; 15:8), and he will "never be shaken" (Psalm 15:5). As a result of his clear conscience, he is open to the testing and judgment of God. Instead of resisting the eyes of the Lord, he invites them.

Guilty men, on the other hand, feel threatened by the scrutiny of God's Word. They get angry at those who hold them accountable. But an honorable man has no fear of things like marital scandal, misappropriation of funds, or little white lies — because none of those are present in his life to take him down. He knows trust is built and gained over a lifetime, but it can be squandered and lost in a moment.

Even when a man of integrity sins, he doesn't deny it, cover up, or hide it. His mode of operation is to confess it, learn from it, and move on, seeking to avoid it in the future.

How would you like that man to be you?

Then don't expect to find moral character fortified in your breakfast cereal or arriving in the afternoon mail. Integrity must be intentionally pursued and courageously guarded, built throughout a lifetime and gained by hard work and sacrifice.

David said, "I kept myself from my iniquity" (Psalm 18:23) and "walked in my integrity" (Psalm 26:1). Day after day. Night after night. To protect his integrity, a man learns to "guide his affairs with discretion" (Psalm 112:5 NKJV). He walks circumspectly according to a moral code of ethics he has established to guide himself. What others claim as tolerable, he knows is too risky.

So if you see a man of impeccable integrity in his old age, you can be sure he made his character a priority over the years. He was careful with whom he spent his time and the men he partnered with in business. He guarded his behavior around other women and didn't allow himself to be put in compromising situations. He refused to cheat on his finances and over the years likely made some people mad who encouraged him to cut corners and compromise.

But you can't help but respect him now. No pretense or façade. What he says is what he means. Both his name and his word are gold. He has sought to be a "doer of the Word" and not a "hearer" only (James 1:22). The Word of God thrives in him because of his "honest and good heart" (Luke 8:15). He has walked with God and let Him open up his life for full inspection, gutting out the dishonesty and replacing it with sincerity.

That word *sincere,* by the way, means "without wax." Ancient sculptors and pottery makers would hide imperfections in their work by pouring wax into the cracks of their fractured merchandise, then painting over the blemishes. After it was sold and used around heat, the wax would melt out, proving the piece to be faulty. But those craftsmen who made reputable products with no fractures would stamp SINCERE on the bottom to show that their work was "without wax" and was the real thing. It was solid. True. It had integrity.

We, too, can only hide our sin and deception for so long. The heat of God's Word and the temptations and trials of life will reveal over time whether we are truly sincere before God or not. Psalm 15 points out the areas where we can test our lives against a man of integrity.

Our relationships. "He does not slander with his tongue, nor does evil to his neighbor, nor takes up a reproach against his friend" (Psalm 15:3). Instead of backstabbing, gossiping, or lying about others, integrity makes us want to build people up and treat them with respect.

Our values. "In whose eyes a reprobate is despised, but who honors those who fear the Lord" (Psalm 15:4). Integrity puts character above wealth, popularity, or position. It causes us to despise deception in our own lives as well as in others, and to honor those who are walking with God.

Our commitments. "He swears to his own hurt and does not change" (Psalm 15:4b). This means we make wise, careful promises — and then keep them even when they're hard to see through to completion. We pay our debts and keep our marriage vows. "Better not to vow than to vow and not pay. Do not let your mouth cause your flesh to sin" (Ecclesiastes 5:5–6 NKJV).

Our price tag. "He who does not put out his money at interest, nor does he take a bribe against the innocent" (Psalm 15:5). A man of integrity can't be bought. He won't allow money to corrupt him. He doesn't underpay his employees or lie on his taxes. He doesn't rob God in his giving. Money doesn't have a hold on him.

He holds on to his integrity instead.

When God looked at Job's life, He could honestly say, "There is no one like him on the earth, a blameless and upright man, fearing God and turning away from evil" (Job 1:8). Even when Job lost everything, even when his wife said to him, "Do you still hold fast your integrity? Curse God and die!" (Job. 2:9), he continued to honor God in the midst of intense suffering, depression, and pain. He heroically said, "As long as my breath is in me, and the breath of God is in my nostrils, my lips certainly will not speak unjustly, nor will my tongue utter deceit. . . . Till I die I will not put away my integrity from me" (Job 27:3–5).

What would happen if we as men began to resolve like Job to walk in total integrity? What would happen if believers in Jesus Christ became known for their honesty rather than being noted for hypocrisy? What needs to happen in your life for this to take place in you? What changes and commitments do you need to make?

There is too much at stake for us not to take integrity seriously. It is for this reason that we end this chapter challenging you to "be careful how you walk, not as unwise men but as wise, making the most of your time, because the days are evil" (Ephesians 5:15–16). Resolve to learn from your mistakes, repent of your sins, and walk in integrity before God.

COURAGEOUS CHALLENGE

Write out a list of the top five sins that keep entangling you in your life, and begin praying for God to give you the grace to fully repent of each one.

MEMORY VERSE

Repent and return, so that your sins may be wiped away, in order that times of refreshing may come from the presence of the Lord. (Acts 3:19)

Create in me a clean heart, O God, and renew a steadfast spirit within me.

Psalm 51:10

Chapter 14
Resolve to Be Found Faithful

I WILL seek to honor God, be faithful
to His church, obey His Word, and do
His will.

Men love glory. We love that feeling we get
from accomplishment, success, and ap-
plause. We love coming in first, being labeled
the best at something. But the problem is
that we want the glory for ourselves.

The paradox is, grabbing for glory and
truly deserving it don't really go together.
The surest way to garner genuine praise is
by working humbly and unselfishly, by acting faithfully and responsibly. The smell of
pride on someone disgusts us. We hate the
thought of their soaking in the spotlight.
It's vain. Jesus said, in fact, that we forfeit
whatever reward we might have received if
we do something solely for others to notice
us.

Don't do your good deeds publicly, to be admired by others, for you will lose the reward from your Father in heaven. When you give to someone in need, don't do as the hypocrites do — blowing trumpets in the synagogues and streets to call attention to their acts of charity! I tell you the truth, they have received all the reward they will ever get.
(Matthew 6:1–2 NLT)

Every time you brag, show off, or fish for praise, you actually *dishonor* yourself. King Solomon said, "Let another man praise you, and not your own mouth; a stranger, and not your own lips" (Proverbs 27:2 NKJV).

But by stepping back and looking at it from a biblical perspective, we realize that honoring ourselves is at best hollow, and at worst selfish and prideful. This is what Scripture refers to as the "pride of life" (1 John 2:16) — trying to do things and possess things so that we can brag in front of others.

Men who take this approach forget that everything good about their lives is really an undeserved gift from God. The apostle Paul wrote, "What do you have that you did not receive? And if you did receive it, why do you boast as if you had not received it?"

(1 Corinthians 4:7). Any accomplishment of yours only happened because you put into practice the strength, opportunities, and abilities God has granted you. If you have made a lot of money, it's only because God has given you the "power to make wealth" (Deuteronomy 8:18). If you are gifted, it was a gift.

So God says:

"Let not the wise man glory in his wisdom, let not the mighty man glory in his might, nor let the rich man glory in his riches; but let him who glories glory in this, that he understands and knows Me, that I am the LORD, exercising lovingkindness, judgment, and righteousness in the earth. For in these I delight," says the LORD.
(Jeremiah 9:23–24 NKJV)

Our lives were actually designed, created, and intended to honor God, not ourselves. Men who live for their own honor are choosing a very, very small thing to live for — themselves. They foolishly praise the painting, not the Painter. The Bible says that God despises pride but gives grace to the humble. He intentionally works in a way "so that no man may boast before God"

(1 Corinthians 1:29).

Creation was His doing. The cross and resurrection of Jesus Christ were His doing. Salvation was His doing. And you were His doing. So it doesn't matter how good a man is at something, or how much he gathers for himself, or how strong he is, or how knowledgeable. In comparison to God, he is nothing. "For if anyone thinks he is something when he is nothing, he deceives himself" (Galatians 6:3).

The Sovereign Maker of everything towers over the microscopic finiteness of "me." This is why we should redirect our focus, our passions, and our energies on what matters most in life, most in death, and most in eternity — God. "Worthy are You, our Lord and our God, to receive glory and honor and power; for You created all things, and because of Your will they existed, and were created" (Revelation 4:11).

So don't settle for trophies that will only collect dust and be soon forgotten. Don't settle for the approval of men when you could gain the approval of God. You have one life to live. And living it for yourself is futile. True fulfillment comes only by gratefully giving God the glory He deserves, knowing that He is the Source of all good things.

Soaking in praise sours us. It rots us over time. Just look at people who soak in their praise as if they deserve it. It only makes them unfulfilled, empty, and more calloused. But anytime we reflect praise back to God and thank Him for anything good we have done, it feels really good . . . and very *right.* We get to share in the joy of being used by Him, and also the blessing of offering thanksgiving and honor back up to Him. It keeps us humble, grateful, and in a place where we are more ready to be used again in the future.

Which is a true honor.

So ask yourself: "Is my life about me or about Him? Is it a picture of honor or dishonor toward God? Do my business practices, actions at church, and goals in life make Him shine or bring Him shame? Am I revealing that I have been redeemed and function as a new man in Christ? Or does everything reveal that I am playing a game and merely deceiving myself with my own façade?

We should freely pray, "Thine is the kingdom, and the power, and the glory forever" (Matthew 6:13 KJV). He owns it all and has accomplished it without us. Therefore, He gets the credit for everything we do because "from Him and through Him and to Him are all things" (Romans 11:36). End of story.

If you're serious about "honoring God" — as the first part of this resolution point says — then lead your heart away from the vain and toward the eternal. Fall out of love with this world and deeply in love with the Lord. Whether you "eat or drink or whatever you do, do all to the glory of God" (1 Corinthians 10:31). He's worthy and worth it.

"I WILL BE FAITHFUL TO HIS CHURCH"

God never intended for you to live out the journey of your spiritual life alone. When you got connected to Christ, you also became spiritually connected to everyone else who is *in* Christ. "We, who are many, are one body in Christ, and individually members one of another" (Romans 12:5). We are permanently joined together and deeply need each other. Whether you are married or single — if Jesus is your Lord, the church is your spiritual family.

And so you need to be "faithful to His church."

You may be new to church. Or you may have been burned by so-called Christians in the past. If so, you're in good company because Jesus' main enemies were the religious, hypocritical "churchgoers" of His day. They were the ones who organized His betrayal and ultimate crucifixion.

All people have been and can be hypocrites in one or more areas of their lives. Inside and outside the church. But don't let churchgoers who do the wrong thing keep *you* from doing the *right* thing. This should never be an excuse to give up on church or not get involved. In fact, it is more of a reason to plug *into* one — because we all need God's help. We all need a spiritual support system of like-minded people on this journey together.

The truth is, none of us has it all together. Please don't think because we are writing this book that we think *we* do. We are far from it and remain very challenged by God's truth as we share it in these pages. That's also why we are so passionate about the church. It is our spiritual support system. All of us need godly people around us so we can learn from one another's mistakes and build one another up. The Scripture tells us to "encourage one another day after day, as long as it is still called 'Today,' so that none of you will be hardened by the deceitfulness of sin" (Hebrews 3:13) — to "bear one another's burdens, and thereby fulfill the law of Christ" (Galatians 6:2).

Churches consist of people like us: sinners who have given their lives to Christ and are learning to walk in grace, love, and truth. That's why the Bible says, "Let us consider how we may spur one another on toward love and good deeds. Let us not give up meeting together, as some are in the habit of doing, but let us encourage one another — and all the more as you see the Day approaching" (Hebrews 10:24–25).

Jesus calls the church His bride. His beloved. His body. He is always working through the church to carry out His purposes throughout the world. He loves her, died for her, and is preparing her for heaven (Ephesians 5:25–27). So if you say you love Jesus but you avoid the church, you're saying to Him, "I love you, but I can't stand your bride."

Wonderful people who love God and love others are among those found in church — people who will cheer for your hopes, encourage your dreams, celebrate your joys, and then stand by you in the emergency room or weep with you at a funeral. They'll give you the shirt off their back, then offer their back to help bear your burdens. God wants all believers in Jesus Christ to stay closely connected with one another. This is where you'll find men with whom to lock shields — men who will sharpen you, challenge you, and fight the battles of life with you.

This is no time to head for the tall grass. If you have been out of church in the last few months, it's time to turn your horse around and get back involved.

Here are four keys to being successful in how you plug into a church:

1. *Show up and get involved.* How can you feel connected, loved, and ministered to if you're never there? Attend consistently, not just every once in a while. And don't sit on the back row on Sunday morning and then jet for your car during the closing song. Get involved in a small group Bible study. Find a place to serve. Don't stand at a distance. Dive in with both feet and join the fun.

2. *Fix your eyes on Jesus, not on people.* Jesus won't fail you, but people will. So give them permission to be human, and forgive them when they disappoint you. Extend the same mercy that you would hope to receive from others. Be hard to offend and quick to forgive.

3. *Be a blessing, not dead weight.* Let love be your motivation for what you do, not merely to be known and loved. Instead of

expecting everybody else to do everything, you do some of the pedaling too. Don't just take. Give. Serve. Encourage. Use the gifts and talents God has given you to be an edifying member of the body. It is what each person contributes that keeps them most connected, "as each part does its work" (Ephesians 4:16).

4. *Finally, share life with other believers.* Invite them into your world. God wants us being part of each other's lives. Challenging one another. Loving one another. Serving one another. Helping one another. Weeping together. Rejoicing together. Doing life together.

The church needs *you,* and you need *them.* God designed it so that as Christians, we multiply one another's joy and divide one another's sorrows. The more we intentionally are knit together with other church members, the more we can celebrate when a member gets married, gives birth, has a prayer answered, gets a job offer, breaks an addiction, or is reconciled to an estranged family member. Their joy is our joy because we are one body.

It's a family sharing in the very joy of God (John 15:11; 17:13), not a country club. It's God Himself, delighting in the unity and good of His people (Psalm 133:1). So invest your life in a Bible-believing, Christ-exalting local church, and increase the joy of others while giving yourself more opportunities to rejoice!

God will match and exceed your faithfulness to the church with His faithful love.

"I WILL OBEY HIS WORD"

In 1756, President John Adams wrote something very profound in his personal diary: "Suppose a nation in some distant region should take the Bible for their only law book, and every member should regulate his conduct by the precepts there exhibited! . . . What a Utopia; what a Paradise would this region be!"

The third element of this vital resolution is about obeying God's Word — the book that tells you the secrets to finding purpose in life, knowing God, building meaningful relationships, wisely handling money, enjoying a great marriage, raising strong kids, and making sense of this fallen world. Yet our culture tends to follow the advice and counsel of carnal men instead, who depend on the shifting tide of political correctness, the current trends, and their own best thinking.

What about you? Do you believe the Bible is just the word of men or truly the Word of

God? The answer to this one question will make a monumental difference in the direction of the rest of your life and in the generations that will follow you.

Yes, the Bible is the most loved *and* most hated book of all time. It was the first book ever published and is translated into more languages than any other in history. And still today, it continues to be the best seller of all best sellers. It is the most read and studied yet most critiqued book of all. But thousands of years of analysis show it still standing strong.

Satan hates it.

Atheists deny it.

Skeptics mock it.

False religions belittle it.

Rebels distort and misuse it.

Why?

Because the Bible is the Word of God. It humbles us, exposes us, and calls us to account. It will befriend you and then blow your mind. It will develop you but also discern the deepest motives of your heart. It is not a dormant, outdated text. It is a living, piercing, "double-edged sword" (Hebrews 4:12). Timeless truth with spiritual power. Not a stagnant pool of rules but a river of revelation.

It explains what's true, what's wrong,

what's right, and what you should do about it.

And not every man wants its bright light shining into his heart.

Almost all religions begin the same way. One man rises up alone and claims in his book to possess divine revelation. But the Bible is not merely one book; rather, it is an entire library of sixty-six books, written by forty-plus authors over a period of 1,600 years, living on three continents, and speaking three different languages. What are the chances they would agree? Yet these books contain historical records, spiritual parables, timeless counsel, songs of worship, and prophetic visions that all unite to tell the complete story of God's redemptive purposes for time and eternity, from beginning to end. Consider them to be bold witnesses in a courtroom, each backing one another up, each verifying the testimony of the other.

More than 330 prophecies in the Old Testament find their fulfillment in the New Testament. The Levitical laws written down by Moses were fulfilled by Christ thousands of years later. Each of the four gospels supports the eyewitness accounts of His life recorded in the others. You can still visit all the places where it took place. The book of Acts connects these gospels to the rest of the New Testament, explaining how the church was birthed and grew from a few disciples to countless transformed followers of Christ. The books of Romans and Hebrews, in particular, contain the theological explanation of God's salvation as seen throughout the rest of the Bible. Every book in the Bible has a unified sense of divine breath and joins perfectly with the others into a tightly woven tapestry that reveals Jesus alone as the way, truth, and life.

The Scriptures are complete. They connect our origins, our history, our morality, our relationships, the nature of God, the way to know Him, and what happens beyond the grave. All of it. All in one place. No book has changed so many lives and so powerfully rocked the world. No book has educated so much ignorance, initiated so much good, propagated so much love, and reprimanded so much evil.

President John Quincy Adams said, "So great is my veneration for the Bible that the earlier my children begin to read it, the more confident will be my hope that they will prove useful citizens to their country and respectable members of society."

More importantly, the apostle Paul said he constantly thanked God that "when you received the word of God which you heard from us, you accepted it not as the word of men, but for what it really is, the word of God, which also performs its work in you who believe" (1 Thessalonians 2:13).

People can say what they want about it, but its historical accuracy, prophetic reliability, corporate unity, and transformational ability all reveal the Bible as the Word of God.

And it is meant to be lived and obeyed.

So don't be intimidated by the mystery of Scripture. Like a mirror, it will reveal the truth about your current spiritual status. But if it reveals you're in a ditch, it will also throw you a lifeline to pull you out. If it reveals you're heading in the wrong direction, it will also become a lamp to your feet and a light to your path. Often when men fall into sin or get confused in life, they'll avoid reading the Bible altogether. But that's like thinking you will drive more carefully at night by turning off your headlights. Nobody would do that.

The ultimate test of faith, however, is not just committing to read it but resolving to do it. You may see a road sign that says, "Warning! Bridge Out Ahead," but if you keep going and don't heed it, you could drive off a cliff. If you read a map with directions to get somewhere but you don't follow it, you shouldn't get mad at God when you become spiritually lost. The Bible is a love letter from God. But if you don't read it and believe it, you may wonder why you'll walk through life feeling unloved.

We must teach our children to read, obey, and apply the Word of God to their lives. This generation is largely biblically illiterate. They think because they can quote John 3:16 and have gone to church for years that they think biblically. But if they are not in the Word constantly, obeying it increasingly, and seeking God daily, they are only deceiving themselves. The discipleship mandate is that we be doers of the Word. We let God's Word determine how we think, speak, and live in every area of our lives. We let it mold us into the image of Christ.

So as a man of resolution, resolve to start spending time with God in prayer and study His Word. Commit to keep reading through the Bible for yourself. Ask God to speak to you each day and then dive in. Then choose to shepherd your family according to its truth.

Faithful men are faithful to the words of the Word!

"I WILL DO HIS WILL"

Jesus said, "I have come down from heaven, not to do My own will, but the will of Him who sent Me" (John 6:38). If we are going to be like Jesus and fulfill our purpose, we must resolve to do God's will, not our own.

The phrase "the will of God" can sound very mysterious, like a code to be broken or a puzzle to be figured out, but it is actually another way to describe "what God wants." His will is described as both a way of living our lives that brings Him the most *pleasure* as well as His master *plan* for our lives that will bring Him the most glory.

When Jesus allowed Himself to be crucified according to the will of God, His sacrifice both brought God pleasure (Isaiah 53:10) and was perfectly according to God's predetermined plan (Acts 2:23).

As we go through life, we will naturally start doing God's will if we are constantly seeking to live in a way that pleases Him, always asking the primary question, "What does God want me to do in this situation?"

Most of His will is already spelled out in Scripture. The more we study His Word and walk with Him, the more we'll discover what pleases Him and the more easily we'll recognize what He wants us specifically to do in any situation for His glory.

And those things that are more directional in nature — which job to pursue, which college to choose, which girl to marry, which house to buy, which church to attend — God will use His Word, His wisdom, His people, and His Spirit to reveal those to us over time as we seek Him.

We already know from Scripture that it is God's will for people who come to Christ to be saved (John 6:40) then become more pure and more like Jesus everyday (1 Thessalonians 4:3). It is His will that we serve others wholeheartedly as unto the Lord (Ephesians 6:6), walk wisely and make the most of our time (Ephesians 5:15–21), and keep praying, rejoicing, and giving thanks in all circumstances (1 Thessalonians 5:16–18). As we do these things over time, God will clarify what His plans are for us.

Whatever God's specific will for your life is, you can know that it will . . .

- line up with what God has already revealed in His Word (Psalm 119:105),
- get clearer over time the more you obey what He's already told you to do (Romans 6:17–18),
- be confirmed over time with peace, renewed passions, and with open doors (Colossians 3:15–4:3), and

- somehow edify the church and help spread the gospel to the lost (Matthew 28:18–20).

Some people are *afraid* to know or discover God's will. They fear they will hate it or it will make them unhappy. But the truth is, it will bring you the greatest fulfillment and purpose in life. It is much better than anything you could come up with on your own. His will is exactly what you would choose if you knew all the facts, had perfect understanding of all things, and were completely loving in your heart. "So then, do not be foolish, but understand what the will of the Lord is" (Ephesians 5:17).

The apostle Paul explained how we can set ourselves up to discover God's will:

I urge you, brethren, by the mercies of God, to present your bodies a living and holy sacrifice, acceptable to God, which is your spiritual service of worship. And do not be conformed to this world, but be transformed by the renewing of your mind, so that you may prove what the will of God is, that which is good and acceptable and perfect. (Romans 12:1–2)

The late Ron Dunn explained (using this passage) that we find the will of God when we present ourselves to God as living sacrifices (even before discovering His will for our lives) and are transformed by the renewing of our minds (by turning away from the world and staying in God's Word). Then we will know the good, pleasing, and perfect will of God.

In other words . . .

PRESENTATION of our lives
+
TRANSFORMATION of our minds
=
REVELATION of His will

And then, when He reveals it, we courageously do it! For His pleasure and for His glory.

What an honor! What a joy to have the Word of God, the people of God, and the will of God impacting our lives and helping us live for the glory of God!

So rise up, man of resolution! Live your life to draw attention and gratitude to the Lord Himself and Him alone. Pour your heart into His people and receive them as your family of faith and mutual support. Stay in the Word and let it renew your mind and transform your life. And before you know it, you'll be doing His will. Not because you have to, but because you'll joy-fully want to. This is living!

COURAGEOUS CHALLENGE

Make a commitment to attend church and a small Bible study group every week for the next month.

MEMORY VERSE

Worthy are You, our Lord and our God, to receive glory and honor and power; for You created all things, and because of Your will they existed, and were created. (Revelation 4:11)

Therefore, my beloved brethren, be steadfast, immovable, always abounding in the work of the Lord, knowing that your labor is not in vain in the Lord.

1 Corinthians 15:58 (NKJV)

CHAPTER 15
RESOLVE TO LEAVE
A LEGACY

I WILL courageously work with the
strength God provides to fulfill this
resolution for the rest of my life and for
His glory.

What would happen if men all over the
world were not only to commit to the *Resolution* but to live it out long-term? What
would happen if millions of children could
see God transform their fathers into tender,
loving dads and powerful, spiritual warriors
who walk in integrity and leave an eternal
legacy? What would it do in the hearts of
our sons and daughters? What would it do
for future generations?

We have written this book because we
want to join God in turning the hearts of
fathers back to their children and the hearts
of children to their fathers.

As you know, we are unapologetically calling men to follow Joshua's example of

spiritual resolve and leadership and say, "As for me and my house, we will serve the LORD." We want to rekindle a vision of what your marriage and family could be like if Christ was completely ruling in your heart and your home. We want you to spend the rest of your life preparing to stand before God and hear Him say, "Well done!"

We have also challenged you to be a chain breaker, a prayer warrior, a justice fighter, and a spiritual mentor — so that your children and grandchildren, as well as the other men around you, will follow your example. Yes, they must decide for themselves. But when your children feel the love of God flowing through your heart into theirs, when they hear the Word of God boldly pouring from your lips, and when they see the power of God at work through your changed life and answered prayer, they will be drawn to know, love, and follow the God of their father.

This is your legacy.

Every father is first to be a faithful follower of Christ, second a faithful husband, third a faithful father, and then a strong spiritual leader in this world. But we must get these in order, starting with ourselves and moving out from there. If we do not love Him first and our wives as Scripture commands, our failure in these areas will greatly limit our success with our children and beyond. But if we are faithful at home, then we can be strong influencers in our cities and nations for Christ. We can positively impact the world ourselves, and then through our children and grandchildren after we are gone.

God has set us up for success. We have a Savior who has reconciled us back to God. We have a heavenly Father who has blessed us with "every spiritual blessing" (Ephesians 1:3). We have new identities in Christ and are accepted and beloved. His divine power has given us "everything" we need for "life and godliness" (2 Peter 1:2–3). We have His Word, His church, His Holy Spirit, and His promises to help us say no to what is evil and not to fear any man or present crisis. He has promised us, " 'I will never desert you, nor will I ever forsake you,' so that we confidently say, 'The Lord is my helper, I will not be afraid. What will man do to me?' " (Hebrews 13:5–6).

But as we approach this final resolution, we must understand something vitally important. If we are not careful, we are still likely headed for failure. We are foolish to think that we will be true to all of these resolutions if we are still relying on our own strength or our own steadfastness.

Here's why . . .

After three years of closely following Jesus, the apostle Peter looked at Christ during the Last Supper and swore to Him with resolution that he would never fall away or prove unfaithful to Him. He declared, "Even if I have to die with You, I will not deny You" (Matthew 26:35). Within a few short hours, however, he had completely failed. Not once. Not twice. Three times he denied he was a follower of Christ. Complete collapse.

Peter was very sincere — just like we can be — when he resolved to be faithful to Jesus. But he was relying on his own strength. Even though acting with great zeal and passion, his pride was mixed into his mind-set, and it set him up for great failure.

The same thing will happen to us . . . unless we humble ourselves and become reliant on God's grace and His Spirit. We must go back to what Jesus said at the very beginning — to the very first words of His very first sermon in the very first gospel.

Blessed are the poor in spirit, for theirs is the kingdom of heaven. (Matthew 5:3)

Becoming "poor in spirit" is a key to living the Christian life daily and fulfilling this *Resolution* long-term. There are many types of poor people. Some wake up needy each morning and have to go out finding work — day laborers — living from hand to mouth in order to survive. Today's work buys tonight's meal. But there is an even more impoverished type of poor — the blind beggar who wakes up hungry every day but cannot work at all. The only thing he can do to survive is to cry out for help. Continually.

This is the type of "poor" that Jesus was describing. But He was speaking of "spiritual poverty," the kind that comes from realizing we are completely powerless apart from God's constant intervention. Helpless on our own.

That's what being "poor in spirit" is all about. It's knowing we can't do anything of eternal value without God's constant help. It's relying completely on Him and begging continually to survive — the extreme opposite of pride and self-reliance.

Think of it. Who was the most powerful, successful, and effective person in the history of the world? Who was the only person who never failed or blew it spiritually? Who was the only one who did the perfect will of

God all the time? Jesus Christ, the Son of God.

And how did He choose to live?

"Poor in spirit."

Constantly, completely reliant upon His Father.

Consider His spiritual poverty. Though He was God, He chose to empty Himself, take on human flesh, and humble Himself as a servant on earth. Jesus was filled with the Holy Spirit and became absolutely dependent upon the Father for all things at all times (Philippians 2:5–10).

He then said . . .

- Not My will, but His will. (John 6:38)
- Not My teaching, but His teaching. (John 7:16–17)
- Not My glory, but His glory. (John 8:49–50; 12:28)
- Not My words, but His words. (John 14:10–24)

He modeled the secret to long-term victory — total surrender of self, total reliance on God. We too, like a hospital patient plugged up to a life support system, must stay intimately connected to Christ and dependent on our heavenly Father and His Spirit for all our spiritual strength, wisdom, guidance, and grace.

The decisions of our lives each day could impact eternity one way or another. We will miss the eternity-wrapped moment of "now" if we are not abiding in Christ. Our selfish nature wants to stay in control and resists reliance on God's Spirit. Our tendency is only to cry out in a crisis when all else fails and we have no other options.

But true power and sufficiency in Christ begins with recognizing our bankruptcy within ourselves. Paul said it is "not that we are adequate in ourselves to consider anything as coming from ourselves, but our adequacy is from God" (2 Corinthians 3:5).

This does not mean false humility or cowardice; it is merely facing reality. This does not mean laziness. God doesn't want you to sit back and coast like He is going to do everything for you. He wants you to call on His name, rely on the strength of His grace, and then wear yourself out six days a week for a worthy cause — Him (1 Corinthians 15:10).

But before you can say, "I can do all things through Christ" (Philippians 4:13), you must acknowledge that "apart from Him I can do nothing" (John 15:5). Then you must learn to "pray without ceasing" (1 Thessalonians 5:17), which means that you

are constantly going to God for the grace
and wisdom you need to be like Jesus and
do His will moment by moment throughout
each day.

"HELP ME, LORD"

We began this *Resolution* journey challenging you to take back the steering wheel —
to reclaim responsibility for yourself, your
wife, and your children. But God never
intended for you to carry the weight of that
challenge alone. He fully intends to carry
you as you carry your family.

He knows you can't keep His commands.
You can't love Him with all your heart,
mind, soul, and strength. You can't really
love your neighbor as yourself. You can't
love your wife with a Christlike love or train
up your children to be mighty on the earth.
You will break all ten of the Ten Commandments, either in action or in your heart, if
left to fend for yourself.

So He calls you to surrender yourself to
Him, allowing Him to control you as you
carry out your responsibilities. His Spirit
constantly puts the hand of God's power
into the glove of your empty, submitted life,
making you a channel of His truth, love,
and grace rather than leaving you to figure
out how to be your own source of strength.

But none of this happens until you finally surrender to His lordship.

The word *Lord* in the New Testament means "supreme master," the one who is really in control. If Jesus is our Lord, then He is the boss who is ultimately in charge. He's the one who makes the decisions. Lordship is when "What does the Lord want?" trumps, "What do I want?"

But coming to this type of commitment is a spiritual journey. You start by believing God exists and realizing that He is who He says He is. Then your belief transitions to faith and trust, placing your life in His hands and following His lead.

But He wants more. He doesn't just want followers. He wants us to surrender ourselves totally to His lordship. Many followed Jesus but then turned away over time when things got tough.

Jesus wants us to give Him all that we are and all that we have for all of our lives. He is not a halfhearted God who is pleased with a halfhearted sacrifice. He wants total, lifelong surrender from you. This is a picture of what true lordship looks like — when there is nothing He could tell you to do that you would say no to. Otherwise He is not your Lord.

But when a man surrenders to the lordship of Christ, God takes him on a journey that tests him and teaches him, calling him to make Christ the Lord over his relationships, his finances, his possessions, his time, his thoughts, his hopes, his everything. Each individual layer that makes up his life becomes the next thing for Christ to control and transform into something of value, beauty, and lasting significance.

Abraham, patriarch of the Old Testament, at first only believed that God existed. But then he was called out to trust Him by faith. Abraham obeyed with childlike belief and launched out, not knowing where he was even going. That was the first step. A big one. But along the way, you can see Abraham learning to trust God with his future, his worship, his wife, his money, and then ultimately his most prized possession: his beloved son Isaac. By the time Abraham surrendered Isaac to God, the Lord knew that Abraham was holding nothing back from Him. God had all of him. Now He could mightily use Him and make him a father of a great nation.

What a legacy! Our future legacy depends on our decisions now.

WITH ABANDON

Jesus is also calling us to hold nothing back. As large crowds began to follow Jesus, He turned to them and boldly said, "If anyone comes to Me, and does not hate his own father and mother and wife and children and brothers and sisters, yes, and even his own life, he cannot be My disciple" (Luke 14:26).

What a shocking statement. What did He mean — "hate" your family?

The word *hate* here means He wants us to love something so much less by comparison (Matthew 10:37). It's not that Jesus wants you to literally hate your family, obviously. We know His main command is to love God, love your neighbors, even love your enemies. But our love for Him must be so complete that the deep love we feel for our family would look like *hate* if stacked side-by-side with it.

That's extreme. But it's exactly right.

The bottom line is that Jesus must be Lord over all of your relationships (Luke 14:26), your possessions (Luke 14:33), and yourself (Luke 14:27). Over everything. He must become the One you are most loyal to. Your most intimate Friend. Because when He is, something amazing happens — something only God could do. *Your love for your spouse, your children, and others actually increases.* He starts loving your family *through* you, far more completely than you could do on your own. When He is Lord, your time, talents, and possessions quit possessing you but start being utilized for God's glory rather than being wasted. He makes you the man of resolution He knows you can only be by living through you.

You may be thinking, "That sure is a lot to ask. It sounds like I'd be giving up everything. I'd be losing my life to do what He's asking of me." *Yes, that's the whole point!* Your life in your hands will only become more and more sinful, eventually burning up like wood, hay, and stubble (1 Corinthians 3:12). But by losing your life in Christ, your life becomes eternally valuable. Jesus said, "He who has found his life will lose it, and he who has lost his life for My sake will find it" (Matthew 10:39). God gave you your life as a trust so you would have something to offer back to Him. Completely. All that you are and all that you have.

This is what lordship looks like. And it is what takes us to a new level.

Consider these seven reasons why you should go beyond belief, beyond merely following Jesus, and wholeheartedly surrender to His lordship:

1. *He already owns you.* The only way to own something is to create it, buy it, or have it given to you. Jesus, our Creator, knit you together in your mother's womb (Psalm 139:13). He *made* you. But not only that, He has *bought* you "with a price" (1 Corinthians 6:20) by shedding His own blood and redeeming you back to God after sin had separated you. His desire is now to own you in every way a person can be owned — by having you *give* yourself fully to Him.

2. *You owe Him a debt of love.* The greatest love ever demonstrated toward you was not your mom birthing you or your wife marrying you, but rather from Jesus Christ. He has loved you by giving you life, breath, food, and shelter, but most of all by looking down on your sin and dying in your place. "Greater love has no one than this, that one lay down his life for his friends" (John 15:13). He paid the greatest sacrifice to meet your greatest need when you deserved it the least. One who would do that is worthy of your life.

3. *You can't handle life on your own.* The Bible describes us as sheep that have gone astray; "each of us has turned to his own way" (Isaiah 53:6). None of us is righteous, "not even one; there is none who under-

stands . . . all have turned aside, together they have become useless" (Romans 3:10–12). Every one of our sins proves that we need His help to make right decisions. Christ must be at the helm of our lives or we are a spiritual train wreck waiting to happen.

4. *He can make you happier than you can make yourself.* By chasing sinful pleasures, we're actually hungering for love, joy, and peace. But these are the fruit of the Spirit, not the fruit of our sins. When we put ourselves first and pursue our happiness, we end up missing God and not being happy either. But when we lose ourselves in the pursuit of loving and pleasing God, then we not only get an intimate relationship with God, but He gives us happiness as gravy on the side. "Delight yourself in the Lord and He will give you the desires of your heart." (Psalm 37:4)

5. *He has your entire life already planned out.* David wrote, "Every day of my life was recorded in your book. Every moment was laid out before a single day had passed" (Psalm 139:16 NLT). And here's why: "For I know the plans that I have for you," declares the LORD, "plans for welfare and not for calamity to give you a future and a hope." (Jeremiah 29:11). "Eye has not seen

and ear has not heard . . . all that God has prepared for those who love Him" (1 Corinthians 2:9). His plans for your life are better than anything you could come up with in a million years. Why not surrender to them?

6. *You will be judged by Him one day.* Though our sins have been forgiven by the pure, perfect sacrifice of Christ — though we are saved by grace, through faith — "we will all stand before the judgment seat of God. For it is written, 'every knee shall bow to me, and every tongue shall give praise to God.' So then each one of us will give an account of himself to God" (Romans 14:10–12). We should never let a day pass that we do not feel solemnly charged "in the presence of God and of Christ Jesus, who is to judge the living and the dead" (1 Timothy 4:1). Why not let the Judge Himself rule our lives now to prepare us for that great day?

7. *He deserves you.* Only Jesus Christ humbled Himself, lived a sinless life, and then took our place on the cross at great sacrifice. The Bible says of Him, "Worthy are You to take the book and to break its seals; for You were slain, and purchased for God with Your blood men from every tribe and tongue and people and nation" (Revelation 5:9). Only Jesus could rightfully

say, "All authority has been given to Me in heaven and on earth" (Matthew 28:18). We don't bow to Him merely because He is asking but because He has earned our allegiance.

So with these seven things in mind, you must ask yourself if there is any reason why you will not surrender all that you are and all that you have to the lordship of Jesus Christ?

Yes, people will misunderstand you for doing this. They will mock and marginalize you. They may even attack and persecute you for the name of Christ. But that won't matter — because it's not about you. Your life is not yours anymore. If you are Christ's, you are hidden in God.

You represent your Lord, not yourself. If they reject you because they have rejected Him, then you don't have to take it personally. Jesus said to "rejoice" if that happens. Celebrate it because "great is your reward in heaven" (Matthew 5:12 NIV).

So whether anybody else supports you or not, surrender your life completely to Him!

You can stay true to this *Resolution* by staying poor in spirit and surrendered to Him, by turning loose and letting Him do it. He'll make you a man who lives seven days a week for the glory of God — not because *you* can, but because *He* can.

Life has always been, still is today, and always will be all about Him. It has never been about us. But we should revel in the awesome privilege of aiming all our passions and the rest of our days at living to bring Him honor. The finale of all things is the glory of God. We don't undertake this *Resolution* so we can brag about our spiritual "awesomeness" or maturity. The goal of being found faithful to our calling is not to be able to show off but to show *Him* off. To make Him famous!

The Bible says, "The eyes of the LORD move to and fro throughout the earth that He may strongly support those whose heart is completely His" (2 Chronicles 16:9). And God's eyes are looking across the earth at this very hour, looking for men who will surrender their all to the One who paid it all — men He will strongly support to step up with courage to be a powerful light and an influential force in our generation.

We need a new generation of men like young David, who will say, "I'm not afraid of the Goliaths in this world who are trying to intimidate us into backing down and staying in the corner. I'm standing firm in the name of the Lord knowing that the battle belongs to the Lord!"

We need an army of men like Nehemiah who will see the desperate needs of the nation and call the men of God to rise up and fight for their marriages, their children, and the next generation. Men who will not only fight injustice and rail against the status quo, but will actively rebuild our families, our churches, and our nations for the glory of God.

We need bold men like Job who, even if we were stripped of our friends, our money, our health, and all the things dear to us, would still say, "The LORD gives and the LORD takes away. Blessed be the name of the Lord. I will not curse God or let go of my integrity. For I know that my Redeemer lives!"

We need selfless men like the apostle Paul, who after making countless mistakes against God, surrendered his life to Christ and lived the rest of his days courageously dependent on God's grace. Men who when beaten and persecuted, cling to God with powerful faith and endurance. Men who when the church needs leadership, say, "Follow my example as I follow the example of Christ" (1 Corinthians 11:1 NIV). Men who will not love their lives unto death but fearlessly look at the future and say, "For me to live is Christ, but to die is gain!" Men who with their final breaths can say, "I have fought the good fight, I have finished the course, I have kept the faith; in the future there is laid up for me the crown of righteousness, which the Lord, the righteous Judge, will award to me on that day; and not only to me, but also to all who have loved His appearing" (2 Timothy 4:7–8).

And most of all, we need a new generation of men like Jesus Christ, the King of kings and Lord of lords, who say to God, "Not my will, but Yours be done!" And at the end of their lives say, "Father, I glorified You on the earth and I have completed the work You gave me to do."

By God's grace, we can each become that kind of man.

A faithful man of resolution.

Now to Him who is able to do far more abundantly beyond all that we ask or think, according to the power that works within us, to Him be the glory in the church and in Christ Jesus to all generations forever and ever. Amen. (Ephesians 3:20–21)

Yes, Lord. Amen!

COURAGEOUS CHALLENGE

Commit alone or with a group of others to be a man of Resolution. Sign your own Resolution print during a special ceremony with your family. (Professionally produced prints are available at courageousresources.com or dayspring.com.)

MEMORY VERSE

Therefore, my beloved brethren, be steadfast, immovable, always abounding in the work of the Lord, knowing that your labor is not in vain in the Lord.
(1 Corinthians 15:58 NKJV)

THE RESOLUTION

I DO solemnly resolve before God to take full responsibility for myself, my wife, and my children.

I WILL love them, protect them, serve them, and teach them the Word of God as the spiritual leader of my home.

I WILL be faithful to my wife, to love and honor her, and be willing to lay down my life for her as Jesus Christ did for me.

I WILL bless my children and teach them to love God with all of their hearts, all of their minds, and all of their strength.

I WILL train them to honor authority and live responsibly.

I WILL confront evil, pursue justice, and love mercy.

I WILL pray for others and treat them with kindness, respect, and compassion.

I WILL work diligently to provide for the needs of my family.

I WILL forgive those who have wronged me and reconcile with those I have wronged.

I WILL learn from my mistakes, repent of my sins, and walk with integrity as a man answerable to God.

I WILL seek to honor God, be faithful to His church, obey His Word, and do His will.

I WILL courageously work with the strength God provides to fulfill this resolution for the rest of my life and for His glory.

As for me and my house, we will serve the LORD.

Joshua 24:15

CONGRATULATIONS ON COMPLETING THE RESOLUTION FOR MEN!

Even as Joshua stood before his family and the people of God and declared his resolution that he was leading his family to serve the Lord (Joshua 24:15), we encourage you to seriously consider setting up a *Resolution* ceremony with other men so you can establish and declare together in front of your families your clearly defined commitments to take responsibility for them and be the spiritual leaders in your homes.

Remember, the *Resolution* is not a promise of future perfection, but a declaration of your desire and commitment to pursue faithfulness by the grace of God. It can have a major impact on you, your marriage, and your children for you to take this courageous step.

Consider inviting your pastor or a spiritual mentor to lead the ceremony and read aloud the *Resolution* points as you commit to them. After you sign your *Resolution,* display it somewhere in your home or office to encourage your family and remind you daily of your commitments.

Then consider taking other men and even your growing sons through the *Resolution* book to help raise up a new generation of strong men who will break the chains in their families and leave a new legacy of faithful spiritual leadership for their children and grandchildren to follow!

May God bless you as you do His will and live for His glory!

APPENDIX 1
HOW CAN I FIND
PEACE WITH GOD?

God created us to please and honor Him. But because of our pride and selfishness, every one of us has fallen short of our purpose and dishonored God at different times in our lives. We have all sinned against Him, failing to bring Him the honor and glory He deserves from each of us (Romans 3:23).

If you claim to be a good person, be honest with yourself and ask if you have ever dishonored God by lying, cheating, lusting, stealing, rebelling against authorities, or hating others. Not only do these sins cause consequences in this life, but they disqualify us from being right before God and living with Him in heaven for eternity. Because God is holy, He must reject all that is sinful (Matthew 13:41–43). And because He is perfect, He cannot allow us to sin against Him and go unpunished, or He would not be a just judge (Romans 2:5–8). The Bible says that our sins separate us from God and that the "wages of sin is death" (Romans 6:23). This death is not only physical; the resulting spiritual death brings separation from God for eternity.

What most people don't realize is that our occasional good deeds do not take away our sins or somehow cleanse us in God's eyes. If they could, then we could earn our way into heaven and negate the justice of God against sin.

This is not only impossible, but it denies God the glory He deserves.

The good news is that God is not only just, but He is also loving and merciful. He has provided a better way for us to have forgiveness and come to know Him.

Out of His love and kindness for us, the Bible says He sent His only Son, Jesus Christ, to die in our place and shed His blood to pay the price for our sins. This provided a pure sacrifice and a just payment to God for our sins and allowed Jesus to receive the judgment we are due. Jesus' death satisfied the justice of God while also providing a perfect demonstration of the mercy and love of God. Three days after Jesus' death, God raised Him to life as our living Redeemer to prove that He is the Son of God (Romans 1:4).

God demonstrates His own love for us, in
that while we were yet sinners, Christ
died for us. (Romans 5:8)

For God so loved the world, that He gave
His only begotten Son, that whoever
believes in Him should not perish, but
have eternal life. (John 3:16)

Because of the death and resurrection of
Jesus Christ, we have been given the opportunity of being forgiven and then finding
peace with God. It may not seem right that
salvation is a free gift. But the Scriptures
teach that God wanted to show how rich
His grace is in showing kindness toward us
by freely offering us salvation (Ephesians
2:1–7). He is now commanding all people
everywhere to repent and turn away from
their sinful ways and humbly trust Jesus for
their salvation. By surrendering your life to
His lordship and control, you can have
forgiveness and freely receive everlasting life.

The wages of sin is death, but the free
gift of God is eternal life in Christ Jesus
our Lord. (Romans 6:23)

If you confess with your mouth Jesus as
Lord, and believe in your heart that God

raised Him from the dead, you will be saved. (Romans 10:9)

Millions of people around the world have found peace with God through surrendering their lives to Jesus Christ. But each of us must choose for ourselves.

Is there anything stopping you from surrendering your life to Jesus right now? If you understand your need for forgiveness and are ready to begin a relationship with God, we encourage you to pray now and trust your life to Jesus Christ. Be honest with God about your mistakes and your need for His forgiveness. Resolve to turn away from your sin and to place your trust in Him and in what He did on the cross. Then open your heart and invite Him into your life to fill you, change your heart, and take control. If you are not sure how to communicate this to Him, then use this prayer as a guide.

Lord Jesus, I know that I have sinned against You and deserve the judgment of God. I believe that You died on the cross to pay for my sins. I choose now to turn away from my sins and ask for Your forgiveness. Jesus, I'm making You the Lord and Boss of my life. Change me and help me now to live the rest of my life for You. Thank You for giving me a home in heaven with You when I die. Amen.

If you just prayed sincerely and gave your life to Jesus Christ, then we congratulate you and encourage you to tell others about your decision. If you really meant it, then you need to take some important first steps in your spiritual journey. First, it is essential that you find a Bible-teaching church and tell them that you want to obey Christ's command to be baptized. It is a great mile marker to share your faith with others and launch your new spiritual walk. Also, plug into your new church and start attending on a regular basis and sharing life with other believers in Jesus Christ. They will encourage you, pray for you, and help you to grow. We all need fellowship and accountability.

Also find a Bible you can understand and begin to read it for a few minutes every day. Start in the book of John and work your way through the New Testament. As you read, ask God to teach you how to love Him and walk with Him. Begin to talk with God in prayer to thank Him for your new life, confess your sins when you fail, and to ask for what you need. Then as you walk with the Lord, He will give you opportunities to share your faith with others. The Bible says, "In your hearts revere Christ as Lord. Always be prepared to give an answer to everyone who asks you to give the reason for the hope that you have" (1 Peter 3:15). There is no greater joy than to know God and to make Him known! God bless you!

APPENDIX 2
SIX POWERFUL INFLUENCES YOU MUST GUARD IN YOUR CHILDREN'S LIVES

As the shepherd in your home, you must "be diligent to know the state of your flocks, and attend to your herds" (Proverbs 27:23 NKJV). That means being fully aware of what is going on with your children, while guiding and guarding the things that influence their hearts and minds. Here are six key influences to constantly keep your eye on. Any of these can steal your children's hearts away from you, pollute their minds, and lead them away from God.

1. *Their friends.* God's Word says, "He who walks with wise men will be wise, but the companion of fools will suffer harm" (Proverbs 13:20). Pray for and surround your children with wise friends. Be willing to say "No" to any parties, sleepovers, and "fun" events that would put your children under the influence of foolish kids. Instead, initiate and lead fun events at your

home and on your turf rather than sending your kids off into unknown situations.

2. *Their education.* The worldviews of your child's teachers in school will likely become the worldview of your child. If you want to raise godly children, you must guard carefully who is teaching them and what is being taught — both at school *and* at church. Homeschooling and Christian schools are worth the sacrifice and should be prayerfully considered.

3. *Their music.* Develop in your children a love for the music of God and a disgust for the music of the world. Teach them to discern if the messages imbedded in music are helpful, loving, truthful, and edifying, or if they are angry, sexual, rebellious, self-centered, or corruptive. Fill their music libraries with godly music performed by godly artists. And lead the way by your example!

4. *Movies/TV.* Today's movies and television shows are now considered two of the top influences in culture. They have become increasingly more influential in how the next generation thinks and interprets reality. Do not let your children watch whatever they want. Build a library of good content, and take time to watch more edifying programs with your kids.

Then discuss afterward what was right and wrong in what you've just seen.

5. *Internet.* With Internet pornography, pedophiles in chat rooms, and an ocean of sites that are stumbling blocks for kids and adults, courageous dads need to become watchmen over what their sons and daughters see online. Train your kids to run from evil, but help them by loading filters onto your computers. At the same time, keep Internet access out of your kids' rooms and out in the open.

6. *Video games.* Video games are often very violent, perverted, and addictive. They are designed to draw your children into a fantasy world and keep them there for endless hours when they could be doing something productive and edifying. Guard what games they play, how long they play them, and be ready at any point to initiate "game fasts" for specific periods of time — even packing up the system altogether if it becomes a stumbling block to your kids.

You can expect each one of these to be a potential battleground. So don't be surprised if your kids momentarily become angry and don't understand why you won't let them be around certain people or be entertained by certain things. *Your love is why!* But remember that saying "No" creates a void you must fill with something better. Lead them toward good friends, good books, good music, movies, and activities. Teach them to ask, "Is this honoring to God?" "Is this true, holy, and healthy?" "Will this help me do the right things?" "Will this make me love God more or less?" "Will this fuel my passion for Christ, or will it pour cold water on it?" Romans 12:21 says, "Do not be overcome by evil, but overcome evil with good."

APPENDIX 3
TEN POTENTIAL CONSEQUENCES OF A MAN WHO COMMITS ADULTERY

The one who commits adultery with a woman is lacking sense; he who would destroy himself does it. Wounds and disgrace he will find, and his reproach will not be blotted out. (Proverbs 6:32–33)

1. *Grieving my Lord.* My adultery would hurt and grieve the One who created me, loves me, died for me, redeemed me, fills me, uses me, sees me, prays for me, will judge me one day, and is preparing a place for me to spend an eternity with Him.
2. *Disgracing the gospel.* I would be dragging Christ's sacred reputation into the mud, becoming a stumbling block to younger Christians and non-Christians alike, causing those who disrespect and hate God to laugh, mock, and blaspheme, while giving them another excuse not to follow Christ (2 Samuel 12:14).
3. *Destroying my reputation.* I would tarnish

my self-respect, as well as the respect and trust of those I love and respect the most. My name would be connected to the shame of adultery with the other men I know who have failed morally and in their marriages.

4. *Breaking precious hearts.* Innocent people would suffer from my decision, like my wife, my children, my parents, and my friends. I would also harm the conscience and relationships of the person with whom I have committed adultery.

5. *Losing priceless possessions.* My marriage could end. I could potentially lose my children's hearts, my friendships could be polluted, my job could be damaged, my heavenly rewards that could have been mine to claim and experience (James 1:12). It would damage years of spiritual preparation through the books I've read, the promises I've made, the training I've done, and others' investments in me.

6. *Poisoning my conscience.* I would be forced to live with guilt that is very hard to shake, with self-condemnation that angers and depresses me against myself, with regret in my mind wishing I could go back and undo it, and with embarrassment anytime it is exposed or brought up.

7. *Forcing God's judgment.* I would experience the harsh discipline He allows into my life now (Psalm 51, Hebrews 12:7–13), as well as the pain of looking Jesus in the face at the judgment seat to give an account of why I did it.

8. *Producing untold shame.* I would bring shame to my wife who married me, to my children who follow me, to my parents who trained me, to my church who share their lives with me, to my friends who care about me, and to those I have won to Christ who have been discipled by me.

9. *Discrediting future effectiveness.* I could disqualify myself to preach the gospel as a pastor, and I would discredit the future trust others have in me.

10. *Creating tangible consequences.* I would be sinning against my body (1 Corinthians 6:18), potentially bringing painful sexually transmitted diseases into my life and marriage from this day forward, causing possible pregnancy with its personal and family implications, and financial consequences that result from all of the above.

For the lips of an immoral woman drip honey, and her mouth is smoother than oil; but in the end she is bitter as wormwood, sharp as a two-edged sword.

Her feet go down to death, her steps lay hold of hell. (Proverbs 5:3–5 NKJV)

APPENDIX 4
SEVEN STEPS TO BETTER SEX

Your level of enjoyment during sex is more about what's going on in your heart, mind, and spirit than in your body. Too often we don't prepare ourselves emotionally, spiritually, and relationally for sex, then we wonder why the act itself is only marginally satisfying. Since the sexual relationship is founded upon your commitment, love, and intimacy, it is important to get all three of these things right before you are physically together.

When a husband and his wife surrender to God completely, love each other fully, and then give themselves to one another wholly, then their intimacy and lovemaking launches to a new level of enjoyment. But not only this, God is greatly glorified in the midst of it all. Here are seven steps to help you take your sex life to a much higher level. Go through these items one by one.

1. *Remove guilt.* Both of you spend a few

minutes in prayer to get completely right *with God* so that no guilt is corrupting or weighing down either one of you. Recommit yourselves to Him and to His lordship over your lives.

2. *Remove bitterness.* Now get completely right *with one another* so that no bitterness exists between you. This means spending some time apologizing and also completely forgiving one another of anything wrong that has come between you. This is vital to bringing about the coming union you both desire.

3. *Remove stress.* Pray for one another and for all the things you've been worried or stressed about. Pray for the future of your marriage and for God to bless your spouse. Prayer brings emotional peace.

4. *Fill up with God's love.* As you're praying, thank God for His love for you, and ask Him to make you a channel of His love to one another. Pray also for God to fill you with His Holy Spirit, that He will pour His love, joy, and peace into your hearts . . . and through you to one another.

5. *Overflow with thanksgiving.* Spend some time now thanking your wife for anything she has recently done for you, then let her do the same for you. Appreciate and value the contributions you make to one anoth-

er's lives.

6. *Pour out affirmation.* Next, verbally affirm your love and long-term commitment to one another. Encourage your wife with things you admire and respect about her, things that still attract you to her. Cherish her with your words, and receive her words of love and devotion for you.

7. *Have selfless sex.* As you start to become physically intimate with one another, both of you make the commitment to focus completely on satisfying the needs and desires of your spouse rather than yourself. Let your love unite in a feast of selfless affection. As you do, worship the Lord with your oneness!

APPENDIX 5
RESOLUTION GROUPS:
ACCOUNTABILITY FOR MEN

All men need accountability. When we know that others are supporting, encouraging, and praying for us, it helps us walk faithfully before God. No man is meant to do this on his own. As members of the body of Christ, we are given different gifts and insights to help us grow and sharpen one another. This is why we urge men to form their own Resolution Groups for continued accountability. The idea of small groups is not a new idea. John Wesley used them more than two hundred years ago. Members of a small group were expected to agree to six common disciplines or commitments. These are recorded in *The Works of John Wesley.* We share them to help you develop your own.

John Wesley's Rules for Groups
1. To meet once a week, at the least.
2. To come punctually at the hour ap-

pointed, not missing without some extraordinary reason.

3. To begin (those of us who are present) exactly at the hour, with singing or prayer.

4. To speak each of us in order, freely and plainly, the true state of our souls, with the faults we have committed in thought, word or deed, and the temptations we have felt since our last meeting.

5. To desire some person among us to speak his own state first, and then to ask the rest, in order, as many and as searching questions as may be, concerning their state, sins and temptations.

6. To end every meeting with prayer suited to the state of each person present.

We encourage you to form a small group of three to seven men with whom you can meet weekly or monthly for encouragement, accountability, and prayer. This may be at your church, home, office, or at a restaurant. The meetings should start and end in prayer, and each man should feel free to share openly and honestly in this safe circle of believers. The goal must be to support, encourage, and strengthen each other in the faith, to help you become faithful men of resolution. Times of accountability should always be motivated by love, and yet be firm and direct when necessary.

Be sure to allow time for others' input and for expressing your thanks to God for the things He is doing. Consider memorizing Scripture and going through good books together. Take time to pray for each other. Once in a while you may want to spend the whole time in prayer. This is where sensitivity to God's guidance is needed.

Choose a leader or someone to get you started each time you meet. Certain ones will need to share more than others on some weeks. But be sure that each man has ample opportunity to speak. Stick with your purpose — you're not here just to socialize but to help each other grow and live for Christ.

If someone is unusually quiet or missing your meetings, it may be his time of greatest need. When we don't feel like sharing or answering questions, that's often when we need help the most. Reach out to each other, *especially* when you sense someone drawing back. Use the list of questions below and on the following page as a guide for keeping one another accountable.

Questions to Ask Initially, then Periodically

1. What are the biggest barriers to your relationship with God?

2. What are the biggest barriers to your relationship with your wife?
3. What are the most serious temptations you're facing right now?
4. What are your greatest points of vulnerability?
5. How can your Christian brothers help you the most in this group?

Questions to Ask Each Other Regularly

If there are more than four or five men involved, keep your answers honest but brief. The point is to regularly bring up each area and thereby give opportunity for sharing and following the Lord's leading. (You may wish to add questions of your own.)

1. What has God shown you recently from His Word?
2. What happened this week/month that put you to the test? How did you respond?
3. How are you doing in your relationship with God? (Be specific — time in the Word, prayer, sense of obedience and dependence on the Lord, etc.)
4. How are you doing in your relationship with your wife? (Be specific — communication, spiritual sharing, conflict resolution, etc.)
5. How are your relationships with your

children or other family members?

6. How are your relationships with others at work, school, or church?
7. How are you doing with your thought life? Did you keep your thoughts and actions pure before God this week?
8. What kind of a ministry did you have this week? Whom did you share Christ with? How did you use your gifts and resources to help and serve those in need?
9. Is there anything else God is convicting you of right now? Have you been truthful?
10. How can we pray for you and support you this week/month?

My Resolution Army

The following is a list of the men I am locking shields with to help me fulfill this *Resolution.* I can call on them when I feel like I'm falling or failing, and they can call on me.

For a righteous man falls seven times,
and rises again. (Proverbs 24:16)

Name _____

Address _____

E-mail _____

Name _____

Address _____

E-mail _____

Name _____

Address _____

E-mail _____

Name _____

Address _____

E-mail _____

Name _____

Address _____

E-mail _____

Name _____

Address _____

E-mail _____

Name _____

Address _____

E-mail _____

Name _____

Address _____

E-mail _____

Name _____

Address _____

E-mail _____

APPENDIX 6
SCRIPTURES TO MEMORIZE
WITH YOUR CHILDREN

Of all the things you want in your children's minds and hearts from now into adulthood, the words of Scripture offer the best guarantee of providing them consistently trusted guidance for every possible situation in life. Especially when introduced at an early age and then reinforced through the years, these verbatim statements from God's Word will stay with them, always available for the Holy Spirit to apply at just the right moment.

Scripture memory scares a lot of men. One reason we don't make it more of an emphasis in our homes is because we don't feel capable of doing it ourselves. But like anything, if you put your mind to it, you can be more capable of memorizing than you realize. When people say they can't do it, they're really just saying they're not willing to work that hard. Set your goals high and make it a priority, and you won't believe how much God can accomplish in you.

So resolve to show your children how seriously you take the biblical challenge to hide God's Word in your heart (Psalm 119:11). Start enjoying the unity it can grow in your family as you commit verses like these to memory together. Let them become what you choose to think on as you drift off to sleep at night, or as you're driving to work or running errands. They'll do a lot more good for you than oldies music and sports talk. And you'll know you're giving your children a trusted inheritance of truth, knowledge, and lasting wisdom.

Look at the following page for a suggested list.

Important Topics

Obeying Parents: Ephesians 6:1–3

Valuing God's Word: Psalm 119:11, 105

Trusting God: Proverbs 3:5–6

Surrendering to God: Romans 12:1; Luke 9:23

Redeeming Your Time: Ephesians 5:15–16

Doing Justly and Loving Mercy: Micah 6:8

Walking in Wisdom: Ecclesiastes 12:1, 13–14

Avoiding Wrong Friends: 1 Corinthians 15:33

Fighting Temptation: 1 Corinthians 10:13

Empowered by Christ: Galatians 2:20; Philippians 4:13

Confessing Sin: Proverbs 28:13; 1 John 1:9

Forgiving Others: Ephesians 4:32

Avoiding Worry: Philippians 4:6–7

Thinking Pure Thoughts: Philippians 4:6–8

Knowing Jesus: John 3:16; 10:10; 14:6; 15:5

Longer Passages
The Ten Commandments: Exodus 20:1–17

The Romans Road: Romans 3:23; 5:8; 6:23; 10:9–10

The Greatest Commandments: Matthew 22:36–40

The Great Commission: Matthew 28:18–20

The Model Prayer: Matthew 6:9–15

The Armor of God: Ephesians 6:10–18

The Nature of Love: 1 Corinthians 13:4–8

The Fruit of the Spirit: Galatians 5:22–23

Whole Chapters
Psalms 1, 15, 23, 91, 139

Proverbs 3

Romans 6, 8, 12

Ephesians 4

Philippians 4

Colossians 1

2 Timothy 2

APPENDIX 7
HOW TO PRAY FOR
YOUR FAMILY

When you think to pray for your wife and children, do you sometimes not know what to say? After you've asked God to bless them and take care of them, do you often just let it go at that?

Yet deep down we know that general prayers are lazy prayers — better than nothing perhaps, but not exactly the kind that show how much we love and care for our family and how dependent we know they truly are on God's grace and power.

The prayer themes on the following pages capture more than two dozen specific requests that come straight from Scripture. We encourage you to look up the accompanying verses and to pray their promises over your wife and each of your kids, inserting specific situations from their lives into your praying, tailoring them to what they're facing or handling at the time. Choose just one line a day maybe, sprinkled throughout each month, rolling them forward into a continuous stream of daily prayer that keeps your heart wanting nothing but God's best for each of them. And as He gives you new things to pray about, add those to your list and keep track of how God responds and answers each one.

Not only does God promise to reward the man who prays persistently with believing faith (Matthew 7:7–8), the heartfelt habit of praying for each member of your family will draw you closer to them, helping you keep your wife and kids at the top of your priorities.

HOW TO PRAY FOR YOUR CHILDREN
Pray that they will . . .

1. Love the Lord their God with all their heart, soul, mind, and strength, and their neighbors as themselves. (Matthew 22:36–40)
2. Come to know Christ as Lord early in life. (2 Timothy 3:15)
3. Develop a hatred for evil and sin. (Psalm 97:10, 38:18; Proverbs 8:13)
4. Be protected from evil in each area of their lives: spiritually, emotionally, mentally, and physically. (John 17:15, 10:10; Romans 12:9)
5. Be caught when they are guilty and receive the chastening of the Lord. (Psalm 119:71; Hebrews 12:5–6)
6. Receive wisdom, understanding, knowledge, and discretion from the Lord. (Daniel 1:17, 20; Proverbs 1:4; James 1:5)
7. Respect and submit to those in authority. (Romans 13:1; Ephesians 6:1–3; Hebrews 13:17)
8. Be surrounded by the right kinds of friends and avoid wrong friends. (Proverbs 1:10–16; 13:20)
9. Find a godly mate and raise godly children who will live for Christ. (2 Corinthians 6:14–17; Deuteronomy 6)

10. Walk in sexual and moral purity throughout their lives. (1 Corinthians 6:18–20)
11. Keep a clear conscience that remains tender before the Lord. (Acts 24:16; 1 Timothy 1:19, 4:1–2; Titus 1:15–16)
12. Not fear evil but walk in the fear of the Lord. (Psalm 23:4; Deuteronomy 10:12)
13. Be a blessing to your family, the church, and the cause of Christ in the world. (Matthew 28:18–20; Ephesians 1:3, 4:29)
14. Be filled with the knowledge of God's will and fruitful in every good work. (Ephesians 1:16–19; Philippians 1:11; Colossians 1:9;)
15. Overflow with love, discern what is best, and be blameless until the day of Christ. (Philippians 1:9–10)

HOW TO PRAY FOR YOUR WIFE
Pray that she would . . .

1. Love the Lord with all her heart, mind, soul, and strength. (Matthew 22:36–40)
2. Find her beauty and identity in Christ and reflect His character. (Proverbs 31:30; 1 Peter 3:1–3)
3. Love God's Word and allow it to bloom her into Christlikeness. (Ephesians 5:26)
4. Be gracious, speaking the truth in love, and avoiding gossip. (Ephesians 4:15, 29; 1 Timothy 3:11)
5. Respect you as her husband and submit to your leadership as unto the Lord. (Ephesians 5:22, 24; 1 Corinthians 14:45)
6. Be grateful and find her contentment in Christ, not her circumstances. (Philippians 4:10–13)
7. Be hospitable and diligently serve others with Christlike joy. (Philippians 2:3–4)
8. Bring her family good and not evil all the days of her life. (Proverbs 31:12; 1 Corinthians 7:34)
9. Have godly older women to mentor her and help her to grow. (Titus 2:3–4)
10. Not believe lies that would devalue her roles as a wife and mother. (Titus 2:4–5)
11. Be loving, patient, hard to offend, and

quick to forgive. (James 1:19; Ephesians 4:32)

12. Have her sexual needs met only by you, and to meet yours. (1 Corinthians 7:1–5)

13. Be devoted to prayer and effectively intercede for others. (Luke 2:37; Colossians 4:2)

14. Guide her home and children in a Christlike way. (Proverbs 31:27; 1 Timothy 5:14)

15. Give no occasion for Satan to accuse and reproach her. (1 Timothy 5:14)

APPENDIX 8
AVOIDING PORNOGRAPHY

No temptation has overtaken you but such as is common to man; and God is faithful, who will not allow you to be tempted beyond what you are able, but with the temptation will provide the way of escape also, so that you will be able to endure it. (1 Corinthians 10:13)

Pornography is idolatry. It creates an addiction of lust that leads a man to surrender his mind, body, money, time, and purity in service to it. It becomes his god and perverted master.

When God created sex for a man and his wife alone to enjoy, He permanently linked its pleasure to marriage, love, intimacy, and lifelong commitment. Each of these keeps the sexual relationship meaningful and reinforces a couple's union in marriage. In holy matrimony, sexual pleasure is grounded in love, freely shared, and maintains its priceless meaning and many healthy benefits. There is no cost. No shame. No guilt. No regrets.

Pornography is the opposite. It strips sexual fulfillment of all its purposes. It disconnects sexual arousal from its foundation of love, marriage, and lifelong commitment, and reattaches it to lust, vanity, irresponsibility, and the perverted thrills of sin and shock imagery. Instead of sexual enjoyment being a reward from God, it becomes an undeserved, unearned, unholy, illegitimate pleasure with no purpose. It is like sexual cocaine that lures a man into a trap and then rapes his mind and conscience, leaving him addicted, numb, and demoralized. He begins caring less about the people he loves. He quits rejoicing over good things and grieving over sin. He feels guilty, dark, and dirty, spiritually distant from God and emotionally disconnected from his wife. Not only that, he also gives Satan a foothold and permission to torment him now with condemnation, lies, and accusations. He's much worse off than when he started.

All addictions create a momentary spike in adrenaline that temporarily feels good but then leaves behind an even deeper void that causes more dissatisfaction than was there before. Because of this, pornography begs you to pursue its short-term thrill again, repeatedly lying to you that its "high" can pull you out of this pit. Lust just keeps breeding more lust. Then you get caught in a cycle that spirals downward and never seems to end.

If you ever feel a ravenous hunger for pornography, realize this: it is the last thing you need, and it will never satisfy you. *Run.* It is trying to use cheap lust to quench your thirst for genuine love. Satan always tempts you to meet legitimate needs in illegitimate ways. What you are actually hungering for is intimacy with God Himself, the only One who can fill the emptiness in your heart. Any lust in us reveals that we have not been feasting on the love from our heavenly Father (1 John 2:15–17).

Countless men have defeated pornographic addictions by learning to walk intimately and obediently with Christ in His Word and in prayer each day. Jesus told the woman at the well, "Everyone who drinks this water will be thirsty again, but whoever drinks the water I give him will never thirst. Indeed, the water I give him will become in him a spring of water welling up to eternal life" (John 4:13–14 NIV). His Spirit can fill and satisfy you in countless ways that pornography never can. So be courageous enough to recognize pornography for what it is: moral sewage and a pit of lies.

- *It lies,* telling you that your sexual pleasure is of higher importance over everything else.
- *It steals,* robbing you of marital intimacy, honor, and future pure enjoyment of the marriage bed.
- *It pollutes,* coarsening your mind, numbing your conscience, and darkening your thoughts.
- *It belittles,* turning people made in God's image into prostitutes, mere sex objects of your lust.
- *It enslaves,* making you feel like you are powerless to stop or control your impulses.

This should disgust us. Look up and study the following verses that tell what else lust does to you. It chokes out the Word in your heart (Mark 4:19); leads you to destroy yourself and degrade your mind (Romans 1:24); causes inner struggle and strained relationships (James 4:1); creates a state of ongoing frustration, anxiety, and dissatisfaction (James 4:2); blinds you to what is most important in life (1 John 2:16–17); and invites the judgment and punishment of

God (1 Corinthians 10:1–6). With these truths and grave warnings in mind, you must resolve before God to walk in complete honesty and purity (1 John 1:7), in full repentance and victory. Scripture shows us how to walk in freedom through the following ways:

- Do not allow lust to rule you anymore. (Romans 6:12)
- Put it completely out of your life. (Ephesians 4:22)
- Set your mind instead on things above. (Colossians 3:1–5)
- Remember that you now belong to Christ. (Galatians 5:24)
- Remember that God's grace empowers you to say "No!" to lust's demands and deceptions. (Titus 2:12)
- Run away when it tries to draw you back in. (2 Timothy 2:22)
- Be like Jesus, willing to suffer rather than sin. (1 Peter 4:1–2)
- Trust the Holy Spirit to fill you, empower you, and help you resist faithfully. (Galatians 5:16-25)
- Escape by believing the promises of God that He will meet your needs and never leave you. (2 Peter 1:4)

God has provided all you need to be completely happy and successful in life (2 Peter 1:3–4). And His plan involves you living free from pornography. If you have been enslaved to it in the past, you know firsthand how low it takes you. God never wants you again to see anyone undressed other than your spouse. Admit this. Human willpower isn't enough. You need God's grace.

So if you are addicted to pornography, confess it to God and someone else in your life who can spiritually hold you accountable (James 5:16). Begin memorizing His Word (like 1 Corinthians 10:13, 2 Peter 1:3–4, 2 Timothy 2:22, Philippians 4:6–8, and Titus 2:12) and using it to fight off temptation. Feast on God each day. He is your source of satisfaction (James 1:17). Get radical about removing things that cause you to stumble (Matthew 18:9). During times of battle, shift your focus to praying for others to distract you from lustful thoughts (Ephesians 6:17–18). Stay accountable to godly friends, and never stop pursuing victory in Christ!

APPENDIX 9
FINAL SPEECH FROM
COURAGEOUS

While writing the screenplay for the movie *Courageous,* we decided to end the movie with a challenge that would inspire men with a portrait of what strong fatherhood looks like. In the movie, one of the main characters, Adam Mitchell, a sheriff's deputy in Albany, Georgia, discovers that he has failed to grasp the vital importance of his role as a dad. After he and his friends commit together to become strong leaders in their homes, they verbally sign the *Resolution for Men* points in front of their families, and then frame and hang it on their walls to help them keep their new commitments. Adam is then invited to speak in front of a thousand people at his local church. He boldly shares the following message that burns in the hearts of the men who hear it.

As a law enforcement officer, I've seen firsthand the deep hurt and devastation that fatherlessness brings on a child's life. Our prisons are full of men and women who have lived recklessly after being abandoned by their fathers, wounded by the men who should have loved them the most. Many of these children now follow this same pattern of irresponsibility that their fathers did. While so many mothers have sacrificed to help their children survive, they were never intended to carry the weight alone. We thank God for them, but research is proving that a child also desperately needs a daddy. There's no way around this fact.

As you know, earlier this year, my family endured the tragic loss of our nine-year-old daughter, Emily. Her death forced me to realize that not only had I not taken advantage of the priceless time I had with her, but that I did not truly understand how crucial my role was as a father to her and our son, Dylan.

Since her passing, I've asked God to show me through His Word how to be the father that I need to be. I now believe that God desires for every father to courageously step up and do whatever it takes to be involved in the lives of his children. But more than just being there or providing for them, he's to walk with them through their young lives and be a visual representation of the character of God, their Father in heaven.

A father should love his children and seek to win their hearts. He should protect them, discipline them, and teach them about God. He should model how to walk with integrity and treat others with respect, and should call out his children to become responsible men and women who live their lives for what matters in eternity.

Some men will hear this and mock it or ignore it. But I tell you that as a father, you are accountable to God for the position of influence He has given you. You can't fall asleep at the wheel, only to wake up one day and realize that your job or your hobbies have no eternal value, but the souls of your children do. Some men will hear this and agree with it but have no resolve to live it out. Instead they will live for themselves and waste the opportunity to leave a godly legacy for the next generation.

But there are some men who, regardless of the mistakes we've made in the past, regardless of what our fathers did not do for us, will give the strength of our arms and the rest of our days to loving God with all that we are and to teach our children to do the same — and whenever possible, to love and mentor others who have no father in their lives but who desperately need help and direction. And we are inviting any man whose heart is willing and courageous to join us in this resolution.

In my home, the decision has already been made. You don't have to ask who will guide my family — because by God's grace, *I will.* You don't have to ask who will teach my son to follow Christ because *I will.* Who will accept the responsibility of providing for and protecting my family? *I will.* Who will ask God to break the chain of destructive patterns in my family's history? *I will.* Who will pray for and bless my children to boldly pursue whatever God calls them to do? I am their father — *I will.* I accept this responsibility, and it is my privilege to embrace it.

I want the favor of God and His blessing on my home. Any good man does. So where are you, men of courage? Where are you, fathers who fear the

Lord? It's time to rise up and answer
the call God has given you, and to
say . . . *I will, I will, I will!*

DISCUSSION QUESTIONS

Introduction and Chapter 1

1) How have you seen the lack of strong fathers affecting this generation? 2) Which of the resolution "I Will" commitments challenges you the most? 3) How has your relationship with your father affected your life? Your view of God? 4) In your opinion, what factors are undermining the influence of fathers? 5) How do you hope this book will help you the most?

Chapter 2

1) What in the parable of James and Timothy meant the most to you personally? 2) In the story, how did James' relationship with Christ affect the direction of his life? 3) How did the story affect how you view your influence as a dad? 4) What ideas did you learn that you plan to implement with your kids? 5) What does it mean to "be like James" — to break the chain and leave a

new legacy?

Chapter 3

1) What chains have been in your family tree or your own home in the past? 2) Have there been any specific sins in your life that your father committed as well? 3) Did your dad deeply love you or deeply wound you? Or both? 4) How does the cross of Christ enable us to break the chains of our past? 5) How can a man break the chain of sin? Hurts? Lies? Bad traditions?

Chapter 4

1) When did you become a man? How did you view manhood as you grew up? 2) What aspects of manhood meant the most to you in this chapter? Why? 3) What areas of childishness have been the hardest to let go as you have matured? 4) How does this chapter affect how you view responsibility? Accountability? 5) How can a father help prepare and call his son into manhood?

Chapter 5

1) What four things did God give Joshua to help him be a successful leader? 2) How does the world's idea of men leading women differ from Christ's servant model? 3) Why is a personal, daily walk with God funda-

mental in helping a man lead his family? 4) What are some things dads would do differently if they took their role seriously as protectors? 5) Did your father lead with love? How will you lead your family with love?

Chapter 6
1) What does it mean to be holy? How does making something holy affect how we view it? 2) What is the difference between "falling in love" and becoming a channel of God's love? 3) Read the consequences of adultery on page 387. How does seeing its dangers listed this way help you? 4) How does it help a man be faithful by first loving God intimately? 5) What boundaries will you put around yourself to guard against pornography and adultery?

Chapter 7
1) What do worldly fathers view as success for their kids? What about godly fathers? 2) What are some things fathers can do to help their children fall deeply in love with God? 3) What are some things your father did that caused him to win or lose your heart? 4) What are the factors of a father's blessing? How did God the Father bless His Son, Jesus? 5) What will you do this week to com-

municate attention, affection, and affirmation to your children?

Chapter 8

1) How can fathers already be teaching and influencing their great-great-grandchildren? 2) What does it mean to fear the Lord? What are the benefits of fearing the Lord? 3) How does God use imperfect authorities in our lives to guide us? 4) Why is it important for fathers to lovingly discipline their children? What are the keys? 5) What tips help fathers teach their children to live responsibly?

Chapter 9

1) What factors cause men to be passive and avoid standing up against evil? 2) What story of a historical justice fighter challenged you the most? 3) How does showing mercy for the hurting go hand-in-hand with fighting for justice? 4) What evils need to be confronted in our day? What battles need to be fought? 5) Close your time together by praying for discernment, hatred of evil, and the courage to act.

Chapter 10

1) How does demonstrating love affect a father's influence in his children's lives? 2) What are the top three "locks" of prayer

that have held you back the most? 3) What "keys" of prayer would you like to practice more? 4) How did Jesus reach out to people who were different from Him? 5) Share about a man in your life you greatly respect. Why do you feel that way about him?

Chapter 11
1) How well did your father provide for you physically, emotionally, spiritually? 2) Why do believers never need to worry about having their needs met? 3) Share a story about how you have seen God miraculously meet someone's need. 4) How does work draw a man away from his family? How can men guard against this? 5) What are some things men do to spiritually lead their families?

Chapter 12
1) How do guilt and bitterness hold a man back from being a godly man? 2) Why is it important to forgive every person who has sinned against you? 3) Read Ephesians 4:26–34. What are the consequences of bitterness? 4) What truths help us to more fully forgive people who have wounded us? 5) Read Matthew 5:23–24. Who do you need to go back to and reconcile with?

Chapter 13

1) What is the difference between how a wise man and a fool respond to failure? To counsel? 2) Why are some things sinful? What are sin's consequences? 3) What is the difference between true and false repentance? 4) What does it mean for a man to resolve to walk in total integrity? 5) What are the rewards of walking in integrity? Close by praying Psalm 19:12–14.

Chapter 14

1) Read Jeremiah 9:23–24. Why do men tend to take glory in the things listed? 2) Why is it important to honor God and not ourselves? 3) What are the four keys to being successful in plugging into a church? 4) How has God's Word impacted you personally? Why is obeying it so essential? 5) Describe the "will of God" in your own words. How does someone discover it?

Chapter 15

1) What is your vision for leaving a strong legacy to your children and grandchildren? 2) Why do some men, like Peter, make commitments but fail to keep them long-term? 3) What does it mean to be poor in spirit? 4) See Luke 14:26–33. Describe the type of commitment that Christ is calling us to? 5)

What are the seven reasons a man should surrender his all to the lordship of Christ? 6) Close in prayer and invite men to surrender their lives completely to Christ.

RESOLUTION NOTES

NOTES

1. Glenn T. Stanton, *FocusFamilyInsight* Global Development Family Research memo, June 19, 2009.
2. Bryan Davis, "Father Facts," All Pro Dad, http://www.allprodad.com/playbook/viewarticle.php?art=375
3. "Turning the Corner on Father Absence in Black America," Morehouse Research Institute and Institute for American Values, The Medical Institute for Sexual Health Update, Fall 1999, Vol. 7, Number 3.
4. "The Consequences of Fatherlessness," Courtesy of the National Center for Fathering, http://www.fathers.com/content/index.php?option=com_content&task=view&id=391
5. Josh McDowell, *The Father Connection* (Nashville: B&H Publishing Group, 1996), 4.
6. Alex and Brett Harris, *Do Hard Things*

(Colorado Springs: Multnomah, 2008), 55.

7. Robbie Low, "The Truth about Men and Church," http://www.fisheaters.com/menandchurch.html

8. http://thinkexist.com/quotation/alexander-caesar-charlemagne-and_myself_founded/262117.html

9. Josh McDowell, "The Vital Role of Fathering," audio message, Focus on the Family Radio Broadcast Ministry, 2005.

10. S. M. Davis, "Winning the Heart of a Rebel," sermon. Delivered at Park Meadows Baptist Church, Lincoln, NE.

11. Allen L. Nell, "The Responsibilities of a Father," http://www.brfwitness.org/?p=565

12. Roland Bainton, *Here I Stand: A Life of Martin Luther* (Nashville: Abingdon Press, 1950), 185.

13. http://thinkexist.com/quotation/cowardice_asks_the_question--is_it_safe/339725.html.

14. Martin Luther King Jr., *Strength to Love* (New York: William Collins & World Publishing, 1963), 33.

15. Charles Spurgeon, *Morning and Evening,* December 28.

ACKNOWLEDGMENTS

We praise God for the following people whose prayers, counsel, encouragement, feedback, and loving support helped make the *Resolution for Men* a reality: our wonderful wives Jill and Christina, our world-changing children, our parents Larry and Rhonwyn Kendrick, our pastor Michael Catt, our Sherwood church family, our book agents and dear friends Bill Reeves and Jim McBride, our faithful and enduring editor Lawrence Kimbrough, our new friend and partner Randy Alcorn (Eternal Perspective Ministries), our friends Ed Litton (Pastor of First North Mobile), Mike Young (Noble Warriors), Jason and David Benham, Trent Pruett, Priscilla and Jerry Shirer, our assistants Kim Sancinito and Marie Keefe, our great B&H partners John Thompson, Thomas Walters, Jeff Godby, Selma Wilson, Cossy Pachares, Thom Rainer, Brad Waggoner, Kim Stanford, Amanda Sloan, and the countless prayer warriors who continue to lift us up and the projects we are working on, and everyone else. We love you and appreciate you!